Mathematical Development

Rebecca Taylor

Publisher's information

Brilliant Publications
1 Church View
Sparrow Hall Farm
Edlesborough
Dunstable, Bedfordshire
LU6 2ES

Tel: **01525 229720**
Fax: **01525 229725**
e-mail: **sales@brilliantpublications.co.uk**
Website: **www.brilliantpublications.co.uk**

Mathematical Development
by Rebecca Taylor
Cover design and illustrations by Ian Hunt

© Rebecca Taylor 2001.

ISBN 1 89765 984

First published in the UK in 2002.
10 9 8 7 6 5 4 3 2 1

Printed in Malta by Interprint Ltd.

The right of Rebecca Taylor to be identified as the author of this work has been asserted by her in accordance with the Copyright, Design and Patents Act 1988.

There are six books in the Foundation Blocks series, one for each of the key areas. Each book contains clearly laid-out pages, giving a wealth of activities, ideas and suggestions. For further details on how these books are structured and how they make implementing the QCA's Curriculum Guidance for the Foundation Stage easy, please see *Introduction* on page 6.

Other books in the Foundation Blocks series include:

Communication, Language and Literacy
by Irene Yates
Encourage children to develop good communication skills, extend their vocabulary, use language to help thinking, begin to link sounds and letters, use and enjoy books and start to develop writing skills.

Creative Development *by Annie Heggie*
Encourage children to explore the different art media and materials available, to recognize and explore sounds, to use their imagination, to express and communicate their ideas, thoughts and feelings using dance, movement, art, music and imaginary play or role play.

Knowledge and Understanding of the World
by Mavis Brown
Contains early years activities for teaching scientific exploration and investigation, early knowledge of technology and information, a sense of time and place and an awareness of other cultures and beliefs.

Personal, Social and Emotional Development
by Mavis Brown
Help children to develop positive attitudes, self-confidence and high self-esteem. Encourage them to form good relationships with peers and adults; to understand what is right, what is wrong and why; and to develop self-care skills with a sense of community.

Physical Development *by Maureen Warner*
Encourage children to move with confidence, control and co-ordination, using a variety of equipment. Help them to gain awareness of space, of themselves and of others and to recognize the importance of keeping healthy.

Contents

Contents

© Rebecca Taylor
www.brilliantpublications.co.uk

Contents

Introduction

- This book has over 100 differentiated activities set in real life contexts relevant to pre-school children (3 to 5 years old). It provides coverage of the Mathematical Development section of the *Curriculum Guidance for the Foundation Stage (QCA 2000)*.

- The activities are divided into sixteen topics commonly used in early years and primary settings. These are:
  - Animals
  - Celebrations
  - Colours
  - Families
  - Food and Shopping
  - Gardening
  - Health
  - Homes
  - Myself
  - People Who Help Us
  - Seasons
  - Shapes
  - Toys
  - Transport and Travel
  - Water
  - Weather

- The topic appears in a shaded box at the top of each page. The other books in this series also use these same topics. While we have suggested topics, they are not set in concrete. All the activities can easily by modified to fit into a topic of your choice.

- These activities will help children to become more confident and competent at all aspects of mathematical development, with many of the activities addressing more than one skill at a time.

Number

- The ability to count is an important aspect of number. Children need to learn not only to say the number names in order, but also to match the numbers to objects counted, know that you say one number for each object you count and that when you count, the last number you say gives you the number of objects in the group.

- Some of the activities in this book will help to develop the child's understanding that numbers can also be used as labels, eg for house numbers, bus routes, television channels, etc.

- Many of the activities contain practical opportunities for calculating, and talking about numbers in everyday situations. Children begin to develop an understanding of addition, subtraction, multiplication and division through comparing and combining numbers of objects, as well as through adding groups of the same number of objects and sharing objects equally between some children.

Shape, space and measurement

- Activities are included to help children develop an understanding of the properties of both 2D and 3D shapes. Children are encouraged to identify and name shapes in the environment.

- The book contains lots of practical activities which involve handling shapes and fitting them together, enabling children to develop an awareness of space.

- Measurement activities in the book provide opportunities for children to compare and order items by length and capacity. The use of a variety of non-standard units of measurement is encouraged. Activities relating to daily routines help children to begin to develop an understanding of time, days of the week and months of the year.

Planning

- All activities include aspects of the Speaking and Listening component of Communication, Language and Literacy. The Personal, Social and Emotional Development area of learning is also included in some activities. Many activities include opportunities for Creative Development.

- Prior knowledge is not expected for any of the activities as the practitioner should choose an activity with the developmental age of the child in mind.

- Although plenary sessions have not been included, it is expected that the practitioner will give time to look back and celebrate what the children have achieved, by talking about it. This adds validity and worth to their work. The children will also learn from others in the group, and this helps to remind them of what they have done.

Logos used on the activity sheets
Box 1 – group size
- This box indicates the number of children recommended for the activity, keeping safety and level of difficulty in mind. Less able children can achieve more difficult tasks with a smaller child to adult ratio. The group size indicates the size of group for the activity itself, rather than for any introductory or plenary sessions.

Box 2 – level of difficulty
- This box uses a scale between 1–5 to depict the level of difficulty the task might present to the children. 1 indicates an activity suitable for children working in the 'yellow band' of the Curriculum Guidance for the Foundation Stage; 5 indicates an activity suitable for able children in the reception class, who are meeting the Early Learning Goals. As most settings have mixed age groups, the majority of the activities have been classified as easy so that the whole class can be involved. Higher levels can be achieved through outcome and the suggested extension activities.

Box 3 – time needed to complete the activity

Safety logo

- This symbol will alert you that adult supervision is required. Where relevant, additional safety notes are included on the sheets. You are advised to read these before commencing the activity.

Safety

- Children are active learners and investigative, exploratory and construction activities invariably involve the use of potentially dangerous equipment. Part of the learning process involves offering the child the opportunities to learn to use this equipment safely. As young children cannot anticipate danger, practitioners have to be vigilant and take part in a regular risk assessment exercise relevant to their own setting.

- Any rules issued by your employer or LEA should be adhered to in priority to the recommendations in this book; therefore check your employer's and LEA's Health and Safety guidelines and their policies on the use of equipment.

Templates

- On pages 118–144 you will find photocopiable templates to be used in conjunction with the relevant activity. The pages are specifically designed to allow children the option of colouring them in. In most cases it is desirable to laminate the pieces, after the children have coloured them, to ensure durability. If the particular piece requires cutting out and gluing, please ensure this is carried out by an adult. Where relevant special instructions appear on the 'template' page.

Links to home

- Where the word 'parent' is used, we refer to all those persons who are responsible for the child, and also include legal guardians and primary carers of children in public care. The 'Links to home' suggest ways in which parents can continue and reinforce the learning that is experienced at the setting.

- Parents can give important information about their children and the child's experiences on which the practitioner can build. It is essential that the practitioner is informed of any health problems, in particular of any allergies.

- Parents can be a valuable resource by giving support when extra help is needed during visits out of the setting, and with more complex activities during designing and making.

- Parents are also a useful source of 'recycled materials' which are required for many of the tasks.

Assessment sheets

Assessment

- Each activity has learning objectives which are linked to the Mathematical Development curriculum.

- To assist the practitioner in their task of planning a balanced programme of experiences, the charts on the following pages show which activities address which of the QCA 'Stepping Stones'. The charts will also be useful for short term planning, identifying future learning priorities and ascertaining whether support is required to achieve a level. The comments column can be used to record comments on the group as a whole, or for individual children. These sheets may be photocopied.

- Other evidence of the child's achievements in the form of (dated) early writing, dictation, drawings, paintings and photographs of 3D work can be kept in a portfolio. This album can also be a source of celebration and pleasure to look at in the future for the child and parent.

- These records should be retained for inspection.

Curriculum Guidance levels: | Yellow | | Blue | | Green | | E.L.G. | (Early learning goals)

Stepping stone	Activities which address stepping stones	Comments
Show an interest in numbers and counting	Pass the animal; Five little Diwali lamps	
Use some number names and number language spontaneously	Bear washing line	
Enjoy joining in with number rhymes and songs	Ten brown bears	
Use mathematical language in play	Christmas shop; Colourful cube game; Animal hospital	
Show curiosity about numbers by offering comments or asking questions	What's your favourite dinner; Creating a post office	
Use some number names accurately in play	The bouncing food café; Bus role play; Birthday shop	

Stepping stone	Activities which address stepping stones	Comments
Willingly attempt to count, with some numbers in the correct order	Sending and receiving apparatus; Who helps us?	
Recognize groups with one, two or three objects	How many wheels?	
Show confidence with numbers by initiating or requesting number activities	Create a garden centre	
Count up to three or four objects by saying one number name for each item	Colour table with a number theme	
Recognize some numerals of personal significance	Number values; The visiting post person	
Begin to represent numbers using fingers, marks or paper or pictures	My animal number book; Teddy bear paper chains How many parts?	
Recognize numerals 1 to 5, then 1 to 9	Our car park	
Count out up to six objects from a larger group	Sorting seasonal clothes	
Count actions or objects what cannot be moved	Let's get physical	
Select the correct numeral to represent 1 to 5, then 1 to 9	How many body parts?	
Show increased confidence with numbers by spotting errors	Our tiger keeps eating numbers!	
Count an irregular arrangement of up to 10 objects	Colour towers; An exciting egg hunt	

© Rebecca Taylor
www.brilliantpublications.co.uk

Stepping stone	Activities which address stepping stones	Comments
Say the number after any number up to 9	Pass the animal	
Begin to count beyond 10	Dressed in your favourite colour; It's an animal day today!; Collecting smiley faces	
Say and use number names in order in familiar contexts	Let's go to market	
Count reliably up to 10 everyday objects	Autumn scales; Making a counting tree	
Recognize numerals 1 to 9	My number book	
Use developing mathematical ideas and methods to solve practical problems	It's our tiger's birthday	
Compare two groups of objects, saying when they have the same number	Pair your favourite socks	
Show an interest in number problems	We have a pet tiger; Making vegetable soup	
Separate a group of three or four objects in different ways, beginning to recognize that the total is still the same	How many cups?	
Sometimes show confidence and offer solutions to problems	Animals in sand and water	
Find the total number of items in two groups by counting all of them	How many wheels?	
Use own methods to solve a problem	How many cups?; How far will my car travel?	
Say with confidence the number that is one more than a given number	Don't forget your toothbrush	

Stepping stone	Activities which address stepping stones	Comments
In practical activities and discussion begin to use the vocabulary involved in adding and subtracting	Multi-coloured playdough; Number igloo	
Use language such as 'more' or 'less' to compare two numbers	How many wheels?	
Find one more or one less than a number from 1 to 10	Pass the animal	
Begin to relate addition to combining two groups of objects and subtraction to 'taking away'	Combining groups of flowers	
Show an interest in shape and space by playing with shapes or making arrangements with objects	Pizza parlour; Design a garden out of shapes	
Show awareness of similarities in shapes in the environment	Design a garden out of shapes	
Observe and use positional language	It's an obstacle race	
Use size language such as 'big' and 'little'	Big animal, little animal	
Show interest by sustained construction activity or by talking about shapes or arrangements	House shape game; Making a piece of furniture	
Use shapes appropriately for tasks	Chinese New Year; The star of David	
Begin to talk about the shapes of everyday objects	Silly toy questions	

© Rebecca Taylor
www.brilliantpublications.co.uk

Stepping stone	Activities which address stepping stones	Comments
Sustain interest for a length of time on a pre-decided construction or arrangement	Construction time	
Match some shapes by recognizing similarities and orientation	Shape swop shop; Shape shop	
Use appropriate shapes to make representational models or more elaborate pictures	Animal homes	
Show curiosity and observation by talking about shapes, how they are the same or why some are different	Sock shapes; Shape collages	
Find items from positional/directional clues	An exciting egg hunt; Hide and seek	
Describe a simple journey	Family journeys; Creating a travel agent's	
Order two items by length or height	Enormous sunflowers; Flower arranging	
Choose suitable components to make a particular model	Animal homes	
Adapt shapes or cut material to size	Countdown to Christmas; Bunny boxes; Make a kite	
Select a particular named shape	Tessellating shape collage	
Begin to use mathematical names for 'solid' 3D shapes and 'flat' 2D shapes and mathematical terms to describe shapes	Animal homes; I spy a shape	

Stepping stone	Activities which address stepping stones	Comments
Show awareness of symmetry	Estimate with cereal; Symmetrical flowers	
Order two or three items by length	I'm the length of that flower!	
Order two items by weight or capacity	Weigh the banana; Autumn scales	
Instruct a programmable toy	Let's be robots; Twist on to a colour	
Use language such as 'greater', 'smaller' 'heavier', or 'lighter' to compare quantities	Autumn scales	
Talk about, recognize and recreate simple patterns	Wrap it up; Repeating-pattern toy; Seaside shop	
Use language such as 'circle' or 'bigger' to describe the shape and size of solids and flat shapes	Silly toy questions	
Use everyday words to describe position	Family photographs; It's an obstacle race	
Use developing mathematical ideas and methods to solve practical problems	We care for our garden; Footstep game	

Any other comments

This activity involves creating colourful number bears for the children to use on a number washing line.

• • • • • • • • •

Resources

- Bear template on page 118
- Thick felt tip pen
- A4 card in two different colours
- Laminate/clear sticky-back plastic
- String
- Pegs
- Pulley mechanism for repositioning the line

Learning objectives

- To have the opportunity to recite numbers in order
- To recognize numbers 1–10
- To identify the missing number

Preparation

- Photocopy the bear template on page 118 on to card and cut it out.
- Draw around the template on alternate pieces of coloured card ten times and cut them out.
- Write a number on each tummy.
- Ensure that all the odd numbers are written on one colour card and the even on the other. Laminate the bears for durability.
- Set your washing line up across a corner of the room where it can be lowered to your children's height when in use.

What to do

- Show the children the bears, asking them what they have on their tummies.
- Pick one bear out and ask a child to peg it up on the washing line where they think it should go.
- Encourage them to use their knowledge of numbers so number 5 would be pegged roughly half way across the line.
- Once all the bears are pegged up ask the children if they are all in the right order. Do any bears need to be moved?

- As a group, say the number names in order.
- Finish by taking all the bears down and hiding one. Peg the bears up placing them in order and then ask the children to guess which is the missing number.
- Repeat several times.

Extensions/variations

- Set the washing line up in your maths area alongside the units where you store your maths equipment.
- On top of your units lay out activities that your children can work on in spare minutes.

Links to home

- Encourage parents to put up a number frieze in their child's bedroom so that the children are stimulated by numbers at home and in the nursery.

Pass the animal

This activity is about organizing a fun circle time that involves the children reciting numbers from different starting points.

• • • • • • • • •

Resources
■ A soft animal of your choice
■ Ball

Learning objectives
● To have the opportunity to recite numbers– in order
● To recite numbers from starting points other than number 1; to count on
● To have the opportunity to co-operate with each other and share the animal

What to do
● Ask the children to sit in a circle.
● Explain to the children that they are going to pass the toy around the circle, counting each pass together.
● Allow the children to pass the animal around while you count up to 10. You can then start again, encouraging them to join in.
● As the children become more confident, start the game by passing the animal but use a different start number other than the number 1, for example 3 or 4.
● Encourage the children to get quicker as they pass the animal.
● You could always clap your hands to encourage a quick response and steady beat.

Extensions/variations
● For higher-ability children you may start on number 5 and encourage them to take away one number instead of adding, for example 5, 4, 3, etc.

● Make the game more energetic by taking it outside and, instead of passing an animal, use a ball. As the children become more confident at passing the ball they could throw it to each other as they count.
● Try to have a number session at the same time every day so that it becomes part of the children's routine.

Links to home
● Encourage the children to repeat the activity at home, with all their family members joining in the counting.
● Have them think about where they and their friends or family can practise counting, for example around the dinner table, or in the car or lounge.

This activity involves the children using 3D shaped junk materials to create a home.

• • • • • • • • •

Resources

- A variety of soft toys
- Large and small boxes
- Tubes of various sizes
- Tissue paper
- Sticky paper
- Newspaper
- Sticky paper
- Material
- Paints
- Glue
- Brown tape
- Masking tape
- Digital camera

• • • • • • • • •

⚠ Adult supervision will be needed when the children are using scissors.

Learning objectives

- To use appropriate shapes to make representational models
- To begin to use mathematical names for solid 3D and 2D shapes
- To adapt shapes and cut materials to size

What to do

- Present to the children a selection of soft animals and tell them that they need homes.
- Talk to them about what a home is and what an animal needs inside their home.
- Some child may suggest it needs a bed or even an 'en suite' toilet.
- Encourage the children to look at the boxes and animals that you have collected.
- Which would be the right box for each animal? Ask the children to put the animals inside the boxes to check for size.
- Once the children have carefully selected their boxes and animals, have them work independently to cut tissue paper, material or newspaper to size for the carpet. They could paint the walls and use sticky paper to decorate them. Inside, they could use smaller boxes to create a bed or anything else that they have suggested.
- You might help the children to cut doors and windows to size in their boxes.

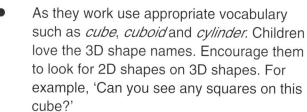

- As they work use appropriate vocabulary such as *cube*, *cuboid* and *cylinder*. Children love the 3D shape names. Encourage them to look for 2D shapes on 3D shapes. For example, 'Can you see any squares on this cube?'

Extensions/variations

- Take a photograph of each child with their finished model (using a digital camera if possible). Have the children talk about their models and say why they like them.
- If possible, encourage the other children to ask questions such as 'How did you make it?'

Links to home

- Put a plea out to parents several weeks before this activity, asking for a variety of junk material.

Animal hospital

This activity involves the children rising to the challenge of caring for sick animals. They will need to count their patients and select the right length bandages.

• • • • • • • • •

Learning objectives

- To have the opportunity to count reliably up to 10
- To count and check in a role-play situation
- To experience different length bandages and use vocabulary such as *This bandage is too long for Teddy's head*

What to do

- In your role-play area let your children help you set up an animal hospital. Collect the resources listed and staple the white backing paper on your screen to create a hospital environment. Make nurse's hats for your children out of strips of white card; cut out a red cross and glue it on the front.
- Write up questions on big pieces of card that will help adults interact with the children in the hospital, such as: *How many patients are there in the hospital today?; How many patients have poorly heads?; How many patients have poorly arms or legs?*
- Work alongside the children, helping them to select the right length bandage for the right job. An arm for example may need a shorter bandage than a head.
- At the end of the session encourage the children to tidy up by checking that all the white shirts are hanging on their hooks, that each 'patient' has its own cushion and

that they are comfortable for the night ahead.

Extensions/variations

- Some children will be able just to tell you how many animals there are in the hospital whilst others might be ready to record the number.
- Provide them with whiteboards and wipeable pens so that they can write their answer and rub it out quickly if they think they are wrong.
- Show some children how to tally as they count.

Links to home

- Find out if any of your parents are nurses who might be prepared to talk to the children about their job and even show how people can be bandaged.

Resources

- Three-sided screen
- White backing paper
- Staple gun, staples
- White and red card
- 10 animals
- 10 cushions
- 6 white adult shirts with the sleeves trimmed to make them manageable for the children
- Large pieces of card
- Thick black felt tip pen
- Bandages of different lengths made out of an old white sheet cut into strips
- Medical bag
- White-boards, wipeable pens
- Telephone
- Appointment book
- Table and 2 chairs for the reception desk

© Rebecca Taylor
www.brilliantpublications.co.uk

Big animal, little animal

This activity involves the children looking through magazines to find big and little animals.

• • • • • • • • • •

Resources

- 2 large pieces of card
- Glue
- Children's safety scissors
- A variety of magazines with animal pictures
- A variety of magazines with pictures of vehicles

Learning objectives

- To use size language such as *big* and *little*
- To have the opportunity to sort animals by size
- To work in a small group, working together to produce a piece of collaborative work

What to do

- Talk to the children about the word *big*. Explain it means that you are talking about size. Can they name any big animals, for example *elephant* or *rhinoceros*?
- Can they name any little animals, for example *mouse*, *bird* and *ladybird*?
- Show the group of children your two large pieces of card. Write *big* on one and *little* on the other. Ask the children to look through the magazines for pictures of big and small animals. When they have found some they should cut them out and stick them on to the right piece of card.
- Encourage the children to talk to each other about where they are sticking their pictures and to share the equipment that they are using.
- When they have finished, encourage the children to recite the names of the animals.
- Can the children think of any other animals that are not in the magazines? Encourage them to draw them.

Extensions/variations

- You might encourage the children to reinforce their learning by repeating the activity but this time changing the theme to vehicles.
- Use size vocabulary in your setting. For example, *Miss Taylor is going to sit on the big chair*, *Lauren is drinking out of the big cup*.

Links to home

- Ask the children to find big and little objects at home. How many big objects can they find? How many little objects can they find?

Ten brown bears

Learning objectives

Class

- To have a secure knowledge of the order of numbers 1–10
- To sing together a number song
- To solve the problem *How many bears are left on the wall when one falls off?*

Preparation

- Paint the box to represent a wall. Make it sturdy. If using template bears, cut them out, letting the children colour them; cut five slits in both of the long sides of the box.

What to do

- Place the cardboard box on the table in front of the children, with the bears on top or in the slots.
- Sing the following song to the tune of 'Ten green bottles':
  Ten brown bears sitting on the wall
  Ten brown bears sitting on the wall
  And if one brown bear should
  *   accidentally fall*
  There'll be nine brown bears
  *   sitting on a wall.*
- After each bear has fallen, stop and ask the children to work out how many bears there are left by counting them.
- As the children sing, encourage them to show the correct number of fingers to represent the bears left on the wall.

Extensions/variations

- You may decide to make ten bear hats that the children can wear. Help the children to paint strips of card brown. Staple the ends together to fit the children's heads and attach brown ears.
- When the bear hats are not in use peg them on to a washing line in your play area.

Links to home

- Ask the children to sing the song at home with their parents, acting it out with their toys. Encourage parents to sing lots of counting songs with their children – it's something they can do wherever they are, such as in the car, shopping or just walking.

Resources

- 10 brown bears or 10 cardboard bears from the template on page 119
- Cardboard box
- Paint and brushes
- Felt tips pens or crayons

Animals in sand and water

This activity will give a counting focus to your sand and water areas.

• • • • • • • • • •

Resources
- Variety of plastic animals
- Plastic trays
- Sand
- Jug for water
- Food colouring
- Washing-up liquid
- Pebbles

Learning objectives
- To count up to 10
- To respond to a problem such as: *If there are four elephants in the sand and one runs away, how many are there left?*
- To work in a small group, sharing the animals, the sand and water tools

What to do
- Place some animals in your sand tray, such as elephants, crocodiles, zebras and camels.
- Work alongside a small group of children as they work in the sand tray, asking questions such as, *How many elephants can you count?*, *Can you dig a hole for four camels?*, *Can you dig a stream for a crocodile to swim in?*
- Make your water area a fun and exciting place to work in by adding food colouring to the water and washing-up liquid to give it bubbles.
- Encourage the children to count how many pebbles they use to make an underwater fun park for the plastic fish.

Extension/variation
- Set the children a theme to their play, such as *Can you make a castle for the elephant?*, *Can you make a playground for the zebras?*

Links to home
- If the children have a sand tray or box at home, encourage their parents to help them create numbers in the sand with their finger or use the end of a spade.
- Encourage parents to make time spent in the paddling pool a fun learning experience. They should ask their child questions such as, *How many cups of water will I need to fill this bowl?*

It's an animal day today

• • • • • • • • •

Learning objectives

- To record as a group what they find out about all the animals that they bring in
- To hear mathematical vocabulary such as, *count, How many altogether?*
- To begin to count beyond 10

Preparation

- Send the following note home to parents:

> *Dear parents,*
> *At the moment, we are learning about animals. We would be grateful if you would allow your child to bring in a stuffed toy animal tomorrow – perhaps a tiger, zebra or bear.*
>
> *We would also like to do animal face-painting with the children in the afternoon. Please would you sign below to give your permission for this activity to take place.*

- Store the children's stuffed animals by pegging them on to your washing line in your maths area. The child can see his toy and will not panic that it is lost.

What to do

- Sit the children in a circle with their stuffed animals on their laps.
- Encourage the children to identify all the different animals that have arrived.
- Ask the children to stand up if they have brought in a tiger.
- Go round counting these children and then say, for example, *We have nine tigers today.*
- Continue for all the other types of animals that have been brought in.
- Perhaps at the end ask the question, *How many animals do we have altogether?*
- On a large piece of card, draw a grid with the types of animals listed on the left-hand side.
- Ask the children to draw their face on a sticky label and then with your help stick it in the right row. Therefore, if they have brought in a tiger they stick their smiley face in the tiger row.
- When the chart is finished, encourage the children to count the faces by touching them.
- Continue your animal day by having a face-painting afternoon.

Extension/variation

- You could repeat this activity with other items that the children bring into your setting. For example, *Let's count to see how many children have shoes with laces.*

Resources

- Letter home to parents
- Large piece of cardboard
- Square white stickers
- Crayons
- Animal shaped paper
- Face paints
- Children's stuffed animals

We have a pet tiger

This activity involves you introducing to your children a tiger who needs a little bit of help with his numbers.

• • • • • • • • •

Resources

- A stuffed toy tiger
- A basket big enough for the tiger to lie in
- Cubes or buttons, something that the children find easy to count
- A sign saying 'Shh, the tiger is sleeping' (place this in his basket)
- Letter home to parents

Learning objectives

- To be introduced to the early skills of estimation
- To realize that the tiger has given a wrong answer and to put it right
- To have a secure knowledge of the order of numbers

Setting up/preparation

- Place the tiger in his basket in your maths area so that the children begin to associate him with numbers and fun.

What to do

- Gather the children in front of you and sit down with the tiger on your lap.
- Tell them that today you are going to help the tiger to learn his numbers.
- Hold in your hand five buttons.
- Encourage the children to predict how many buttons are in your hand.
- Count them together to see if anyone's prediction was close.
- Ask the children to cover their eyes. Tell them that the tiger is going to take some of the buttons and that they are going to try to work out how many buttons he has taken.
- At first pretend the tiger has taken just one button, so you show the children the four buttons left in your hand. Work up to him taking two, three or more.

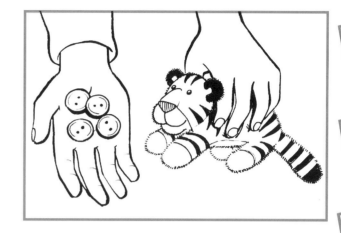

Extensions/variations

- Have the tiger take turns with the children when they are counting. For example, the tiger would say 'two' and they would say 'three' the tiger would say 'four' and they would say 'five'. Make sure the tiger makes mistakes sometimes so that the children have to correct him.
- Ask the tiger questions such as, 'Which number comes before three?' Make sure he makes many mistakes.

Links to home

- Send a letter home to parents: *We have a new pet toy tiger in our setting. We should be grateful if you and your child would think about a name for our tiger and send it in on a piece of paper tomorrow. We will then have a vote to decide the final name.*

My animal number book

This activity involves the children making their very own number book that they can look at again and again.

• • • • • • • • • •

Learning objectives

- To begin to represent numbers using marks on paper
- To recognize numerals 1–9
- To develop hand control by cutting out pictures and tracing over

What to do

- Present to the children a variety of counting books.
- Talk to them about what they notice about them. They often show the number and then a selection of objects to represent that number.
- Explain to the children that they are going to make their own animal number book.
- On the front cover write in yellow writing *My number book* and encourage the children to trace over the top of it with pencil.
- On the first page draw the number 1 with a high-lighter pen so that the children can trace over it. Encourage the children to find and cut out one animal, such as a cat, and stick it on the page. You could write *one cat* on the page.
- Continue this process to number 9.
- Some children may stop at 5 while others may keep going to 9.

Extensions/variations

- For older children you may decide that they do not need to trace over your numbers and that instead they can independently form the numbers using number cards to help.
- They also may like to draw pictures of animals rather than cutting them out and sticking them in.
- Place the finished books in a box in your maths area so that the children can look at each other's.

Links to home

- Encourage your parents to take their children to the local library on a regular basis and borrow counting books.

Resources

- A variety of counting books
- Long strips of sugar paper folded into zig zag books
- High-lighter pen
- Magazines and wrapping paper featuring animals
- Scissors
- Number cards
- Glue
- Pencils
- Crayons

It's my birthday today!

Celebrate every child's birthday in your setting in style.

. . . .

Resources

- Birthday table with a special cloth
- Helium balloons
- Boxes wrapped up with brightly coloured wrapping paper
- Template on page 120 for birthday chart and badge
- Felt tip pens
- Sticky-back plastic
- A list of children's birthdays
- Children's names on cards
- Box to put names in
- Blu-tac®
- Matches stored in a safe place
- Hole punch
- Long pieces of ribbon
- Tin with thick candles stuck on it to represent a birthday cake

. . . .

⚠️ Care needs to be taken when using candles/matches In front of children.
Be aware of nut allergies.

Learning objectives

- To learn how to mark special moments in time like birthdays with a special routine
- To learn about ages, and that birthdays are annual and each time children are a year older

What to do

- Prepare a special birthday table in your setting. Cover it with the cloth, tie the balloons and ribbon to it and place the presents on top.
- Photocopy the birthday chart on page 120, colour it, cover with sticky-back plastic and stick it above the table.
- Make sure a list of the children's birthdays is in an accessible place for you or other members of staff to see.
- Write each child's name on a piece of card and put them all in a little box with some Blu-tac® and place on the table. Cover cards with sticky-back plastic for durability.
- Photocopy the badge on to card, hole-punch and thread a ribbon through, long enough to go round the child's neck.
- When it's a child's birthday encourage them to find their name in the box and stick it on to the chart.
- Give them the badge to wear and display any of their cards on the table.
- Gather the children together and say that there is a very special person here today who has a birthday.

- Sing to them and then clap how old they are counting all together. You might want to give them an extra clap for luck.
- Then present the lit 'birthday cake' to them, encouraging them to make a wish before blowing out all the candles.
  Great care is needed when using candles and matches.

Extensions/variations

- Ensure that you include all members of staff in your birthday routine, although you might want to change it slightly to exclude wearing the badge or clapping how old they are.
- Have a writing table in your setting where children can go in spare minutes to make birthday cards. Make sure you provide examples of number cards on the table so they can write numbers on their cards.

Links to home

- Decide with your staff your policy on children bringing in cakes or sweets to celebrate their birthday.
- Because of nut allergies, many settings have decided to say no to sweets and cakes. However, sharing sweets among friends is a valuable maths activity.
- Whatever your decision, be sure to inform parents by writing it in a newsletter or your setting's prospectus.

Birthday balloons

This activity involves the children learning about the months of the year.

Learning objectives
- To learn the month of their birthday
- To begin to develop an understanding that birthdays are celebrations that come around once a year
- To be able to count the number of children that have a birthday in a particular month

Preparation
- Cut out 12 large balloons from your bright card, making sure that they are all the same size.
- Attach string to the bottom edge with sticky tape.
- Stick a month card on to each balloon.

What to do
- Show the balloons to the children and say the months of the year in order.
- Ask the children to think about which month their birthday is in. Some children have a really good idea, such as it's just before Christmas, or it's when the hot weather is here. For others you will have to look on your list and tell them.
- Encourage the children to draw their face on a sticky label and then help them to put it on the balloon that is the month of their birthday.
- Cover the balloons in sticky-back plastic, so that they last longer. Stick them up in a horizontal line, so that the children know the months follow on from each other.

Extensions/variations
- Make sure you get all members of staff to draw their faces and put them on the right balloon.
- Ask the children questions about the balloons, for example: *How many children have their birthday in January?*, *Which is the most popular month to have your birthday in?* Encourage the children to respond to your questions by touching the balloons.

Links to home
- Encourage the children to find out the birthday months of members of their family. Do any have their birthday in the same month?
- Encourage parents to talk to their children about the passage of time saying, for example, *Today is Monday and the month is April.*

Resources
- 12 large pieces of brightly coloured card
- String
- Sticky tape
- Months of the year written on individual cards
- White sticky labels, one for each child and the members of staff
- Pencils
- Crayons
- Sticky-back plastic

This activity involves you working with your children to create an exciting role-play area.

• • • • • • • • •

Resources

- Easel, or other board for teacher to write on
- Three sided screen
- White backing paper
- Staples
- Stapler
- Poster paints
- Two tables
- Used birthday cards
- Used wrapping paper
- Till
- Plastic money
- Balloons
- A4 card
- Envelopes
- Large card
- Large strips of card
- Felt tip pens

Learning objectives

- To show confidence by initiating a number activity in a role-play situation
- To begin to develop an understanding that we celebrate birthdays by sending cards, giving presents and having parties
- To handle money in a role-play situation

What to do

- Gather the children in front of you and ask them to tell you what they think a birthday shop should sell. Write the items as a list on your easel. How many can they think of?
- Gather a group of willing helpers and set up your birthday shop in your role-play area.
- Set up your three-sided screen and staple white backing paper on to the walls.
- Encourage the children to paint balloons on the paper. *Can they paint three red balloons? Can they paint two blue balloons?*
- Set up one table at the front of the shop and place on it the birthday cards, wrapping paper, till and money and tie on the balloons.
- At the back of the shop set up a table where the children can make birthday items such as cards, birthday hats and birthday banners.
- Put up a big sign that says 'Birthday Shop'.

Extension/variation

- Put some questions up in your birthday shop that will help members of staff interact with the children while they are working, for example: *How much are your birthday cards?*, *How many balloons do you have for sale?*, *Would you be able to make a birthday hat that will fit my head?*

Links to home

- Encourage your parents to allow their children to handle money at home, perhaps by giving them pennies to count and make towers with.
- Encourage the children to talk about how they celebrate birthdays in their family and which shops they visit to buy presents and cards.

Countdown to Christmas

Learning objectives

- To learn that Advent is a special time of the year when we count down to Christmas
- To cut shapes out of circles and experience halves and quarters first hand
- To paint a picture of a snowman that has a repeating-pattern scarf

What to do

- Show the children a variety of Advent calendars and tell them that they are all going to work together to create a class Advent calendar.
- Work out how many days in December that you have left in your setting. You may just want to count down to your last day rather than to Christmas Eve.
- Photocopy the snowmen on page 121 or ask the children to paint their own snowman, encouraging them to paint a repeating colour pattern on his scarf, for example red, blue, red, blue.
- Give the children some white circles and show them how to fold them in half and then in quarter.
- Help them to cut shapes out of their circle and then open them to reveal their very own special snowflake.
- Using your number templates and red card cut out the numbers that you require.
- Once the snowmen are dry cut them out and stick a number on to each one.

- Stick a front of a Christmas card on to the back of each snowman.
- Using your letter stencils cut out on white paper the words 'Countdown to Christmas'.
- Put up your pale blue backing paper and staple a till receipt roll all the way around the edge. Paint a zigzag all the way round.
- Blu-tac® the words on to the top of the display. Pin snowmen on to the display, mixing up the order of the numbers.

Extension/variation

- Each day in December, ask the children which number snowman you should turn around. Get them to guess what might be behind the snowmen. Could it be a Christmas tree, Father Christmas or a Christmas pudding?

Links to home

- Encourage the children to talk about what is behind the doors of their Advent calendar at home.
- Have the children count how many Christmas cards they have in their house. How many trees, how many presents under the tree and how many baubles?

Resources

- Illustrations on page 121
- A variety of Advent calendars
- Poster paint
- Brushes
- Sugar paper
- White paper cut into large circles
- Red card
- Templates for numbers
- Used Christmas cards
- White paper
- Templates for letters
- Pale blue backing paper
- Till receipt roll
- Glue
- Blue-tac®
- Scissors
- Staples
- Staple gun
- Drawing pins

⚠ Care should be taken when the children are using scissors.

This activity involves creating a shop that will pull in the crowd.

• • • • • • • • • •

Resources

- Three sided screen
- White backing paper
- Poster paints
- Brushes
- 2 tables
- Used Christmas cards
- Used wrapping paper
- Till
- Plastic money
- Boxes
- A4 card
- Tree stencil on page 122
- Green card
- Tissue paper
- Envelopes
- Large card
- Large strips of card
- Felt tip pens
- Stapler
- Staples

Learning objectives

- To show confidence by initiating their own number activities in a role-play situation
- To begin to develop an understanding that Christmas Day is a moment in time that we celebrate in a variety of ways, such as sending cards, giving presents and having special food
- To handle money

What to do

- Gather the children in front of you and ask them to think about what they would expect a Christmas shop to sell. Remind them of the birthday shop they made.
- Gather a group of willing helpers to set up your Christmas shop.
- Set up your three-sided screen and staple white backing paper on to the walls.
- Encourage the children to paint two Christmas trees on the paper. Can they paint three red Christmas presents? Can they paint three yellow stars?
- Set up one table at the front of the shop and place on it Christmas cards, wrapping paper, a till and plastic money.
- At the back of the shop set up a table where the children can wrap boxes, make Christmas cards, Christmas crowns and decorate Christmas trees with balls of tissue paper.
- Put up a big sign that says 'Christmas Shop'.

Extensions/variations

- To help the children make Christmas trees use the stencil on page 122. Cut it out twice on green card and make a slit 'up' one and a slit 'down' the other. Push the trees together so that they are ready for the children to decorate with rolled-up balls of tissue paper stuck on to represent baubles.
- Invite parents to participate in this activity. Display questions in the shop that will help other adults to interact with the children, such as *How many days are there left before Christmas?*

Links to home

- Provide a list of children's names to help everybody write their Christmas cards.
- How many Christmas cards are they going to send?

Five little Diwali lamps

This activity involves the children making five little lamps to burn on their window sill to welcome Lakshmi, the goddess of wealth.

• • • • • • • • •

Resources
- Plasticine
- String of beads that are usually draped around Christmas trees
- Scissors
- Nightlights
- Thick playground chalks

Learning objectives
- To practise counting skills
- To learn about the Hindu festival of light known as Diwali, celebrated in Oct/Nov
- To learn how to mould clay into a sphere and then make a thumb hole

What to do
- Find out if any of your children have any friends, neighbours or relatives who celebrate the festival of Diwali, and who might be able to visit your setting and talk to your children.
- Show the children how to make a little lamp holder by moulding Plasticine into a sphere and making a hole with their thumb big enough to take a nightlight candle.
- Cut up the string of beads and show the children how to press the beads into the Plasticine. Tell them that they can only use ten beads for each lamp.
- Show them how to lightly press the base of their candle holders so that they sit on a table. Repeat until they have five little lamp holders and can count them. They will make a lovely display on their lounge windowsill.

Extensions/variations
- Many Hindus use chalks to draw rangoli patterns outside their homes on the pavements to welcome visitors. Rangoli patterns are usually very bright and symmetrical and have lots of shapes in them.

- Encourage your children to experiment in your outside area, using playground chalks to make their own rangoli patterns. They will certainly welcome any visitors to your setting.

Links to home
- Ask the children to find out if they have any candles in their homes. When do they light the candles? Perhaps they are lit at special family celebration dinners.

This activity involves your children making straw triangles to create a very important symbol.

• • • • • • • • •

Resources

■ White art straws
■ Sticky tape
■ String
■ Paints
■ White A4 paper
■ Green garden sticks

Learning objectives

● To learn about the properties of a triangle
● To discuss the importance of symbols in everyday life and in other religions and cultures

What to do

● Encourage the children to think about the symbols that you have in your setting. For example you might have the symbol of a smiley face to represent good work and good behaviour whilst a sad face might be a symbol of unacceptable behaviour.

● Talk to the children about how religions use symbols. For example, the Jewish religion has a symbol called the Star of David as it represents the shape of King David's shield.

● Show the children how to make a triangle by bending a long white straw into three and then joining it with a clear piece of sticky tape. Repeat to make another triangle and then place on top of each other and move around until a star shape is formed. Secure with more pieces of sticky tape. Hang up your Stars of David with a piece of string.

Extensions/variations

● Many countries put their religious symbols on their national flag. Young children are always fascinated by flags and enjoy

looking at flag books. Provide them with white paper, paints and green garden sticks and encourage them to make their very own flag, which might have circles triangles or smiley faces all over it.

● Have a flag-waving parade.

Links to home

● Encourage the children to bring in something from their home that is a symbol of their religion, but remember some families may not be religious. Christians, for example may bring in a symbol of a cross or a fish. Japanese people have the Shichi-go san symbol. Chinese people have the dragon as a symbol.

Chinese New Year

Celebrate this very special festival by making a sparkly spiral decoration.

• • • • • • • • •

Resources

- A4 red card
- Templates on pages 123 and 124
- Scissors
- Gold thread
- Gold paint
- Paintbrushes
- Glue
- Wool
- Pretend cooking equipment
- Chinese take-away menus
- Price lists
- Chinese calendars
- Red paper
- Plastic money

Learning objectives

- To learn about the Chinese New Year festival
- To learn that circles can be cut into spiral shapes

What to do

- Find out if any of the children have Chinese friends, neighbours or relatives, who may be prepared to talk to the children about how they celebrate New Year.
- Explain to the children that Chinese people celebrate the start of their New Year around February. It is a time when they do much cleaning and have specially prepared meals with their families. They decorate their houses with decorations and lanterns.
- Show the children a Chinese snake spiral that you can hang around the room.
- Help the children draw around a circle on a piece of A4 red card and cut it out.
- Encourage the children to paint dots and spiral shapes all over their card using the gold paint. When it is dry the child should paint the other side.
- When both sides are dry cut into a spiral shape and hang up with gold thread.
- Hang them over a radiator so that the children can watch them moving and twirling.
- Show the children how to make Chinese lanterns (see page 123).

Extensions/variations

- Set up a Chinese take-away in your home corner. Wool makes great noodles and the children will really enjoy frying it in a pretend wok. Your local take-away may be prepared to provide you with price lists, menus and Chinese calendars that you can display on the walls.
- Show the children how to make little red envelopes and fill with plastic money. During the festival many Chinese people give gifts of money wrapped in red envelopes to each other.
- Make Chinese dragon face masks and fortune cookies (see template pages 123 and 124).

Links to home

- Encourage the children to talk about visiting their local Chinese take-away. Did they see any special decorations hanging inside? What does Chinese food taste like?
- How do the children celebrate New Year with their family?

This activity involves creating a shop that will pull in the crowds.

• • • • • • • • •

Resources

- 10 cut out cardboard eggs
- 10 cardboard gift box eggs that you can buy from most card shops
- Cubes
- Plate of hot cross-buns
- Stuffed toy Easter bunny
- Stuffed toy Easter chick
- Used Easter cards
- Vase of daffodils
- Cardboard for signs
- Thick felt tip pens
- A letter home to parents explaining about the Easter bonnet parade
- Prizes if desired for the parade

Learning objectives

- To find and count up to ten eggs
- To be introduced to the early skills of estimation
- To help each other as they search for eggs

What to do

- Set up an Easter table in your setting using the items listed in the resources so that the children know that the festival is approaching.
- On the day of the hunt put up a big notice on the door of your setting saying *This is the start of the egg hunt. Can you find ten eggs that look like this?* Stick an example of the egg next to the sign.
- Having hidden the eggs all over your setting in fairly visible places, let the fun begin!
- If you have an outdoor area you may decide to continue the search outside with egg-shaped gift boxes. These are better outside because they do not blow away. Hide them in safe places such as in the back of large toy trucks or by flowerpots.

Extensions/variations

- Give two children cardboard gift-box eggs filled with cubes. Ask the children to pretend that they are chocolates.
- Ask the children to estimate who has the most cubes. Encourage each child to count their cubes to see if their estimation was correct.

- Place the eggs on your Easter display table so that the children can look at them and remember what they have done.

Links to home

- Send a letter home to parents telling them that you intend to have an Easter bonnet parade and that you would like them to work together with their child to create an Easter bonnet. There is lots of measuring in this activity because the child and the parent will have to check that the bonnet fits and that any ribbons are long enough to tie under the child's chin.

Bunny boxes

This activity involves the children experiencing a real-life practical problem: 'How are we going to share these eggs?'

• • • • • • • • •

Learning objectives

6–8

- To decorate bunny boxes with two eyes and one nose
- To experience how shapes slot together
- To use developing mathematical ideas and methods to solve practical problems

What to do

- Make the bunny box on page 125 in advance to show the children what their box will look like.
- Help them to decorate the bunnies, reminding them that each one needs two eyes, one nose and one mouth.
- Have them turn the box over and repeat on the other side. How many bunnies are there altogether?
- Show them how to fold the bunnies along the dotted lines and then how the arms slot together.
- Encourage the children to choose their favourite colour tissue paper and put it inside the box.
- Put the boxes on the Easter table and tell the children that if they are very good the Easter bunny might come along and fill them. You will find that the children will keep checking their boxes.

Extension/variation

- On the last day before Easter in your setting put the big bag of mini eggs on your Easter table with a note from the Easter

bunny. Tell the children that you do not know how to share them fairly. Do they have any suggestions? The idea that everyone sits in a circle and that you put one in each bunny basket, then if there are any left, you go round again so that every one has two, might have to be prompted.

Links to home

- Encourage the children to share the eggs with their family. How many eggs will each member of his or her family get?
- Encourage parents to do hunts at home. It could be a sock-and-shoe hunt. Explain to parents that it is a great way to develop the children's counting skills.

Resources

- Large sheets of white card
- Bunny box template on page 125 (draw around the templates and cut them out for the children, as they are quite fiddly)
- Crayons
- Pencils
- Scissors
- Circles of tissue paper
- A large bag of mini eggs to share amongst the children
- Easter table as on page 33

© Rebecca Taylor
www.brilliantpublications.co.uk

This activity involves the children creating their very own piece of repeating-pattern wrapping paper.

• • • • • • • • • •

Resources
- Sheets of wrapping paper as example
- Large pieces of sugar paper
- Poster paints mixed with PVA glue to make it thicker and better for printing
- Trays
- Shaped sponges
- Large boxes
- Sticky tape
- Different objects to go inside the boxes to make them light or heavy (place the boxes in your maths area so that the children can lift them, placing them in order by weight)

Learning objectives
- To show curiosity by talking about patterns: *How are they the same?*, *Why are they different?*
- To create a simple piece of patterned wrapping paper

What to do
- Show the children a variety of pieces of wrapping paper. Can they identify the patterns, such as red balloon, green balloon and red balloon?
- Can they identify any shapes on the paper, such as square, circle or triangle?
- Set the children up with their large pieces of sugar paper.
- Encourage them to select two different sponges and two trays of paint.
- Help them to create one line of pattern across the top of the paper, such as red circle, green triangle, red circle, green triangle.
- Keep saying the pattern vocabulary to them as they work.
- Once they have done one line of the pattern, encourage them to start the next line and keep going until the whole sheet is covered.

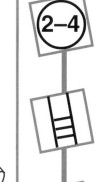

Extensions/variations
- Once the sheets are dry, help the children to wrap their boxes.
- Encourage the children to count the shapes in their patterns. How many red circles have they used? How many green triangles?
- If you have a house in your role-play area, you may decide to allow the children to print a repeating-pattern wallpaper.

Links to home
- Ask parents to donate large boxes and used sheets of wrapping paper.
- Ask the children to be pattern detectives in their own home. Is there a pattern on their curtains, shower curtain or wallpaper? Can they spot any shapes in the patterns?

It's our tiger's birthday!

This activity involves the children helping to organize a party.

● ● ● ● ● ● ● ● ●

Learning objectives

● To develop mathematical ideas and methods to solve practical problems
● To count out objects from a larger group
● To learn about marking specific moments in time such as birthdays with a party

What to do

● Tell the children that it's your pet tiger's birthday soon (they should by now have given it a name).
● Ask the children what they think they should do to help 'Tiger' celebrate his birthday. Write all the suggestions up on your easel, ensure the list includes a party.
● Tell them that you think a party would be a good idea.
● Make a list of all the jobs that jobs have to be done before you can have a party, such as work out how many people you want to invite, decide on a day and a time, write the invitations, write a shopping list, buy the food, make the food, set the table, decorate the room, decide how many party games you are going to have. The list should be endless!
● Help the children write invitations to their toy animals, who will be the guests.

Extensions/variations

● On the day of the party, involve the children in the preparations as much as possible.

It's my birthday today

● They could help make the sandwiches and perhaps fruit salad, and help set the table. Can they count out the right number of plastic cups? Does everyone have a knife and fork? How many serviettes do we need?
● Have Tiger's birthday party but then make sure that the children help with the clearing up. Have we wiped up all the plates?

Links to home

● Ask parents if they would be prepared to donate food to the party such as sandwiches, biscuits, little cakes and bottles of squash.
● Encourage the children to talk about their own birthday parties. How many guests did they have? Was there enough food to go round?
● Using the template on page 126, make tiger face masks for the children to wear.

Resources

■ Large paper to write all the plans on
■ Paper to write invitations on
■ Food
■ Plate
■ Cups
■ Bowls
■ Serviettes
■ Knives and forks
■ Birthday banner
■ Balloons
■ Big table and chairs
■ CD player
■ Music
■ Equipment for party games
■ Tiger template on page 126
■ Orange and black paints
■ Paper plates

Colours

This involves the children being really busy counting colours.

• • • • • • • • •

Resources

- Letter home to parents – in your letter you might want to limit the number of colours the children choose to wear, for example red, green, blue, yellow, orange and pink
- Hoops for the children to jump in
- Large piece of card
- Plate to draw around
- White stickers
- Thick black felt tip pen
- Objects in your setting that represent the colours that your children are wearing
- This activity is best done in the summer so that the children can wear brightly coloured T-shirts and shorts

Learning objectives

- To record as a group what they notice about the colours that everyone is wearing
- To hear mathematical vocabulary such as *count* and *how many altogether?*
- To count beyond 10

What to do

- Send a letter home to parents, informing them of the date for your colour theme day. (Make sure every member of staff wears their favourite colour.)
- Sit the children in a circle and put all the hoops in the middle.
- Ask all the children who are wearing red to jump into the hoop. Let the children count how many of them are in red. Repeat for all the other colours.
- Draw around the plate on your piece of card using the felt tip pen to represent the hoops that the children have just jumped in.
- Give each child a sticker and ask them to draw themselves in their favourite colour.
- Write a colour word in each circle and help the children to stick themselves in the right one.

Extensions/variations

- Gather the children in a circle and in turn ask them to say which colour they are wearing.

Class

- Then ask all the children wearing one particular colour to find something in the room that is also that colour.
- Encourage them to think about all the different things they could find. Does it have to be an object? Could it be their friend who is also dressed in that colour?

Links to home

- Ask the children to find out how many red things they have in their house, or how many green.
- What colour is their car? Do any of their friends have the same colour car?

Colour table with a number theme

Learning objectives

- To talk mathematically as they interact with the colour table
- To count up to ten everyday objects
- To match object shapes

What to do

- Find a table in your setting where you can set up your colour display.
- You might decide to choose one colour per week, your display could last for at least ten weeks if you choose, for example, red, blue, yellow, green, pink, orange, purple, brown, black and white.
- Put an easel on the table with a large piece of paper and write on it, 'Can you draw ten red objects?'
- Put a hoop on the table and write a sign saying, *Can you find ten red objects and put them in this hoop?*
- On a piece of card, draw around some red objects such as a tomato, an apple, a fire engine, a red bucket and a red crayon.
- Put the objects in a red basket on the table and then encourage the children to match the object to the shape on the card.
- Repeat this routine for all the colours.

Extensions/variations

- You might decide to organize the children into colour groups.

- Make a name chart with detachable Velcro® names for each group so that they can self-register themselves every morning.
- Encourage the children to count the names in the morning. How many children are here from the red group today?

Links to home

- Encourage parents to help their children interact with the colour display. Are there any objects at home that the children could bring in to add to the colour of the week display?
- Encourage parents to let their children independently find their name card in the morning.

Resources

- Table
- Easel with large drawing paper
- Hoops
- Card
- Thick black felt tip pen
- Coloured objects, for example red objects could be: a tomato, an apple, a fire engine, a crayon and a bucket
- Large piece of card for name chart
- Velcro®

Colour towers

This activity involves the children building towers with a great mathematical focus.

• • • • • • • • •

Resources
- Coloured blocks
- Large wooden blocks to use in outside area
- Books about colours to be stored in reading corner

Learning objectives
- To use mathematical language in play
- To count or select up to six objects from a larger group
- To count an irregular arrangement of up to ten objects

What to do
- Present the children with a box of coloured blocks.
- Can they count out of the box six red blocks?
- Can they carefully build a tower with the blocks?
- Can they count out ten yellow blocks?
- Can they make a repeating-pattern tower by selecting two colours of blocks?
- How many blocks do you need to make a tall tower?
- When the towers fall down, can the children count the irregular arrangement?
- Having given a number theme to their play, encourage them to ask each other to make towers using different numbers of bricks.
- Have the children put an irregular arrangement of blocks on the carpet and get their friend to first estimate how many are there and then count them.

Extensions/variations
- In your outside area have big wooden blocks that the children can use to make structures.
- Ask questions such as *How many bricks do you think we need to make a house?*
- Make comments such as *I wonder how many wooden bricks there are altogether.*

Links to home
- Encourage parents to take every opportunity to count with their child. Count their Lego® as they put it away. Count the teddies on their bed. Count the wheels on a car.

Multi-coloured playdough

• • • • • • • • •

Learning objectives

- To have an opportunity to talk mathematically as they take part in a daily activity in your setting
- To realize the importance of counting when cooking, for example, *1 cup of flour*, *2 tablespoons of oil*

What to do

- Have the children wash their hands and then help you to collect the ingredients that you need from the resources list.
- Get the children to help you put the flour, salt, cream of tartar and oil into a large saucepan, stressing the counting as they do it.
- Add the food colouring to the water.
- Add the liquid gradually to the ingredients in the saucepan, giving each child an opportunity to stir the mixture to get rid of as many lumps as possible.
- Send the children off to another activity whilst you put the saucepan over a medium low heat and cook, stirring constantly. The mixture will suddenly thicken.
- Continue to stir until the dough becomes very stiff. Remove the pan from the heat and scrape out the dough with a wooden spoon into a bowl. Let it cool.
- Take out to the children and allow them to knead it well.

Extensions/variations

- Hold regular playdough-making sessions and build up a store of colours. Store in polythene food bags inside an airtight box or jar.
- Make every effort to have regular cooking sessions in your setting to capitalize on all the maths opportunities that they provide.
- Make sure you make savoury items as well as sweet, for example vegetable soup, pizza, cheese straws and bread rolls.

Links to home

- A great fundraising activity is for parents to contribute their favourite recipes to a class recipe book that you could sell.

Resources

- 1 cup of flour
- 1/2 cup of salt
- 2 teaspoons cream of tartar
- 2 tablespoons oil
- 1 cup of water
- A few drops of food colouring
- Have a special area in your setting which is set aside for food preparation
- Always stress to the children that the utensils used here are for food preparation only.

Construction time

This activity involves the children spotting shapes in their constructions.

• • • • • • • • •

Resources

- A variety of construction materials such as: Lego®, Duplo®, Mobilo, Polydrons and blocks
- Junk modelling items such as boxes, tubes
- Different pieces of material
- Polaroid camera
- A table

• • • • • • • • •

Make sure that you rotate your construction time so that it is not always available to the children. They will have a new interest in the Lego® if they have not seen it for a while. Make sure all construction material is labelled and that the children know where to get it from and where to put it back.

Learning objectives

- To talk about the shapes that they see in their models and how they are arranged
- To learn self-importance

What to do

- Have 'construction times' on a regular basis so the children have the opportunity to build models independently or in groups.
- Always encourage sharing, and stress that the construction materials belong to everyone.
- Provide the children with a piece of material to make their model on as this ensures construction materials are not spread all over the carpet.
- Work alongside the children as they make their models, asking questions such as: *Why are you putting that cone on top of that cube?, Tell me how you made that model?, Why have you put that cube there?*
- When the children have finished their models, take photographs of them with a Polaroid camera if possible. The children will love watching the photo develop.

Extensions/variations

- Create a table where the children can display their models. Encourage them to write their name on a sign or label to go next to their model.
- Discourage the children from fiddling with the other children's models, as there is nothing worse than a collapsed model!

Links to home

- Encourage the children to build models at home. If they think they have made a good one, could their parents take a photograph of it, so it could be brought in to your setting.
- You could have a notice-board in your setting, showing the kind of things your children do at home. Photographs of their models could be displayed on it.

Colourful cube game

Learning objectives

- To take turns and begin to develop an understanding that sometimes you might lose a game
- To recognize and respond to the numbers on a die by moving the appropriate number of places
- To know that a die is a cube

Preparation

- Photocopy the game on page 127. Colour and laminate it.
- Photocopy the die on page 128. Colour the appropriate circles, laminate for durability and fix it together.

What to do

- Gather a small group of children together, explaining that today they are going to play a colour game.
- Show them the die and the board. Ask them what colours they can see.
- Decide who is going to start. The die is thrown and the child says which colour it has landed on and moves their counter to the next square of that colour.
- The winner is the first one to the finish.

Extensions/variations

- If you are able to paint your outside area, large board-game designs such as snakes and ladders always interest the children, but make sure you use special outdoor paints.

- Provide the children with a foam die and encourage them to be the counters.
- Paint a hopscotch board and perhaps a number caterpillar that the children can move along.
- If painting is not possible, you can always make grids for the children in chalk.

Links to home

- Encourage parents to play board games with their children at home, for example snakes and ladders, Ludo and Mousetrap®.

Resources

- Template of board game on page 127
- Template of cube on page 128
- Felt tip pens
- Laminating material
- Sticky-back plastic
- A large table
- Store all your games in your maths area and ensure an adult always joins a group when a game is being played to encourage fair play and positive behaviour

This activity involves the children actively responding to instructions.

• • • • • • • • •

Resources

■ 3 red cardboard circles
■ 3 blue cardboard circles
■ 3 green cardboard circles
■ 3 yellow cardboard circles
■ Laminator
■ Twister dial on page 129
■ Split pin

Learning objectives

● To respond to instructions given by a robot
● To make different shapes with their body

Preparation

● Cut out the cardboard circles and laminate them so that they can be wiped after being used outside.
● Photocopy the twister dial on page 129. Colour and fix the arrow on to it.

What to do

● Lay the cardboard circles out as a grid in your outside area. Play this game in groups of three or four. Decide the order of play and twist the dial.
● Say in a robot voice, *Claire, put a hand on a red circle*.
● Twist again for the next player and say, for example, *Martin, put a foot on a green circle*.
● That game ends when there is only one child left. Play a final for all the winners.

Extensions/variations

● Alternatively, lay the cardboard circles in a long line to make a 'stepping stones' game.

● Ask the children to start in different places along the line and then say: *Everyone, move forward one place*, *Everyone, move back two spaces*, *Everyone, move forward three places*.

Links to home

● Encourage parents to help their children to count things that cannot be touched, such as jumps, skips and hops.

Number values

Learning objectives

- To talk about and record numerals of personal significance
- To say number names
- To begin to represent numbers by drawing them in the air and writing them on whiteboards

What to do

- Gather the children into a circle and tell them that today they are going to talk about numbers that are important to them.
- Talk about numbers which are important to you, for example your age and date of birth, your shoe size, your house number, your phone number, your car registration number, the number of people in your family, how many brothers and sisters you have, your lottery numbers, your lucky number.
- You might not want to disclose all these numbers to the children but it is important for them to know that numbers are a part of everyday life.

Extensions/variations

- Encourage some children to record by showing fingers or drawing numbers in the air.
- Have other children record their numbers on whiteboards, showing them how all numbers must start at the top.

- Make signs that show significant numbers in your setting, such as: *We have 6 aprons*; *We have 30 pencils*.

Links to home

- Encourage parents to teach their child, their address. If they are able to, it is very useful to remember their own telephone number.
- Send home a letter every term for parents to update their contact numbers if necessary.

Resources

- Whiteboards
- Wipeable pens
- Large easel
- A4 card
- Large felt tip pen
- Letter home to parents

This activity involves creating a role-play area with the focus on the number 3.

• • • • • • • • • •

Resources

- The story of Goldilocks and the three bears
- Three-sided screen
- White backing paper
- Poster paints
- Brushes
- Material
- Kitchen appliances
- 3 plates
- 3 cups
- 3 bowls
- 3 sets of knifes and forks
- 3 teddy bears
- Doll
- 3 bear hats (you could use the ones that you made for the song 'Ten brown bears' on page 119)
- A blond wig for Goldilocks
- Plastic food
- Boxes from tea bags, cereals, eggs
- Tea towel
- 3 aprons
- Vase of artificial flowers

Learning objectives

- To show confidence by initiating number activities in a role-play situation
- To count everyday objects such as three spoons, three dishes
- To work in small groups

What to do

- Gather the children in front of you and read the story of Goldilocks and the three bears. Ask them to show with their fingers how many bears there were.
- Tell the children that you are going to have the three bears cottage in your role-play area. List the objects that the children think should be in the kitchen.
- Gather a group of willing helpers to set up your cottage.
- Set up your three-sided screen and staple white backing paper on to the walls.
- Encourage the children to paint a repeating pattern on the paper to create wallpaper.
- Staple material up at the window to represent curtains.
- Move in the kitchen table and have the children set it for the three bears.
- Move in the kitchen appliances and add the finishing touches such as putting a tea towel by the sink and perhaps a vase of flowers on the kitchen table.

Extensions/variations

- Work alongside your children in the cottage, perhaps taking on the role of Goldilocks.
- Encourage them to re-enact the story of the three bears, cooking the porridge and then deciding to go for a walk in the forest.
- Bring a number focus into the story, such as Little Bear was five years old and he had four best friends.

Links to home

- Encourage parents to give their children little jobs around the house, such as laying the table, pairing the socks after they have been washed, tidying up their bedroom, helping you walk the dog. A reward of a smiley face for each job, could be introduced. When a certain number of smiley faces have been collected, the child could have a treat of their choice.

Family journeys

This activity involves a travelling toy that loves to go on family journeys.

• • • • • • • • •

Learning objectives

- To talk about journeys made, such as a trip to the shops or a trip to Scotland
- To begin to develop an understanding of the passage of time, for example the time it takes to travel to Scotland or Land's End

What to do

- Introduce the travelling toy to your children by showing them photographs of you with the toy at local places of interest. It might be the local park or forest, or it might be at your house.
- Describe each journey explaining the mode of transport and how long it took.
- Send the letter home to parents, explaining that the children can borrow the toy.
- When the children come back with the toy, encourage them to talk about their journey and how long it took them. A child with a good understanding of the duration of time might say, 'We left after breakfast and we did not get there until bedtime. It was a very long journey.'
- You might like to create a graph with the help of the children, which shows how many times the toy has been in a plane, car or train, or has walked.

Extension/variation

- Set up a board in your setting which is dedicated entirely to the travelling toy.

Place on it maps, postcards and photographs that describe the journeys that it has made. Put a display table next to it, where you can place a globe, and perhaps artefacts that the toy might bring back from its journey, such as shells, ornaments and guide books. Write in a scrapbook every time a child borrows the toy.

Links to home

- Letter home to parents.

Dear parents,
We have a very special toy that likes to go on family journeys. Your child is very welcome to borrow him and take him on holiday or to visit relatives. If it is possible, we would be very grateful if you would take a photograph of your child and the toy at your destination.

Resources

- Photographs
- Letter to parents
- Travelling toy
- Display board
- Display table
- See page 130 for display ideas
- Backing paper
- Till roll for border
- Poster paints
- Scrapbook
- Maps
- Globe
- Postcards
- Pictures

© Rebecca Taylor
www.brilliantpublications.co.uk

Family photographs

This activity involves the children using positional vocabulary to describe their family snaps.

• • • • • • • • •

Resources

- Letter home to parents
- Children's photographs
- White paper
- Pencils
- Crayons
- Display board
- Card
- Thick felt tip pen

Learning objectives

- To use positional vocabulary such as *I am next to my Mummy, My Daddy is behind me,* and *My dog is in front of me*
- To use size vocabulary such as *My Daddy is bigger than me*

What to do

- Send a letter home to the children's parents, asking for their child to bring in a family photograph on a certain day.
- Gather the children into a circle and ask them to each hold up their photograph.
- Ask children to walk around the circle showing their photograph.
- Then ask them to describe it to the other children, using vocabulary such as *next to, behind, in front of* or *above*.
- Ask questions to encourage them to describe the size of people in their photograph: *Who is the biggest?, How many people are in the photograph?, How many ladies and how many men?,* and *How many children?*
- Display the photographs on a board with a sign saying 'Our families'.

Extensions/variations

- Ask the children to try to draw their family photograph, making sure they include all their family members.

- Can they show size in their picture? Does their Daddy look bigger than they do? Does their dog look smaller than they do?

Links to home

- Be very sensitive of family circumstances. Everybody's family is special. Some families consist of just two people, whilst others may have three, four or more people in them.

Pair your favourite socks

Learning objectives

- To compare two groups of objects and say when they have the same number
- To use number language, for example *one*, *two*, *lots*, *hundreds*, *how many?*
- To use size vocabulary

What to do

- Sit the children in a circle and put a huge pile of socks in the middle.
- Have the children work together to pair the socks up.
- Ask questions such as: *How many socks are there altogether?*, *How many socks are there in a pair?*, *How many pairs have you made?*, *How many pairs of blue socks have we made?* and *How many pairs of pink with black spots?*
- Use size vocabulary, for example *These are big socks. I wonder who these belong to?* or *These are little socks. I wonder who these belong to?*
- Encourage the children to get into pairs themselves. Can they pair the animal toys together next time they play with them, just like the animals did as they went into Noah's ark?

Extensions/variations

- Have a sock wash day, with the children washing the socks in the water tray. Have the children help fill the water tray. How many buckets do they think they will need?

- Ask the children to help you peg the socks up on a washing line in your outside area. How many pegs do they think you will need?

Links to home

- Ask parents to donate any old socks that they no longer require. You can use them for this activity and they also make great hand puppets.

Resources

- Lots and lots of pairs of socks, which are different colours and different sizes
- Water tray
- Washing powder
- Washing line
- Pegs

Sock shapes

This activity involves the children feeling for shapes and discussing shape properties.

• • • • • • • • • •

Resources
- A variety of socks
- A washing line at the children's height so that they can feel the socks
- 2D plastic shapes
- 3D wooden shapes
- Old box
- Wrapping paper
- Material and cord string to make a feely bag

Learning objectives
- To use shape and position language, for example *Which shape will fit in this sock?*
- To hear you describe properties of shapes, for example *It has four straight lines and four corners. I think it is a square*

What to do
- Set up in front of the children a washing line, and peg on a variety of socks containing different shapes.
- Say to the children that you wonder what is inside the socks.
- Put your hand in, feel, and say, *Oh, I think it is a shape and it has three corners and three sides, I wonder if anyone can guess what shape I am feeling?* Help them towards the answer that is a triangle.
- Repeat for the next sock, describing the properties and ask the children to guess what shape is inside.
- Ask a child to take on your role and describe the shape they are feeling.
- Display the socks in your setting, so that your children can go to them in spare minutes and play the game.

Extensions/variations
- As well as socks for this feeling activity, you could use a feely bag or a feely box. A feely bag is better if it has a drawstring at the top and perhaps a felt face on the front to motivate the children. A feely box can be made by covering an old box with bright wrapping paper and cutting a hole large enough to fit a hand through at the top.
- Instead of using 2D shapes, you could use 3D shapes.

Links to home
- Encourage parents to use mathematical language with their child to discuss shapes in their environment, for example *same because; different because; curved; has corners.*

Family number session

Learning objectives

- To share their maths knowledge and vocabulary with their parents in a different context from their home
- For parents to be informed of the number work that you do in your setting and have the opportunity to ask questions

What to do

- Plan this session carefully with all members of staff.
- You may decide to start off with a whole-group activity, for example Sock shapes, and then move the children on to group activities. These could include: working in the three bears' cottage, playing the 'Colourful cube game', or using the multi-coloured playdough to cut out shapes and make 3D shapes such as cylinders and cubes.
- Some parents may not realize the vital maths work that is happening and will really appreciate it if you talk to them about the learning that is going on in each activity.
- Perhaps have a drink and biscuit halfway through, with the children counting out the cups and thinking about how they are going to share the plate of biscuits.
- Finish with a whole-group number activity such as 'Pass the animal' and praise the children for all their hard work.

Extension/variation

- If the session is successful and well received, you may decide to hold a literacy session that parents can attend.

Links to home

- Send a letter home to parents' inviting them to work alongside their child in your setting for perhaps an hour or an afternoon.

Resources

- Letter to parents
- Equipment for the activities
- Cups
- Juice
- Biscuits

My family number game

This activity requires the children to design their own game and to play it.

• • • • • • • • •

Resources

- Board game template on page 131
- Die template on page 132
- Glue
- Sticky-back plastic
- A box of dominoes

Learning objectives

- To use mathematical language when playing a game
- To begin to develop an instant recognition of one, two or three spots on the die
- To take turns

Preparation

- Photocopy the number track and die on pages 131 and 132 for every child.
- After the child has coloured in the dots on the die, cover with sticky-back plastic to make it last longer, cut it out and glue it together.

What to do

- Provide each child with a number track and encourage them to decorate them with members of their family. Perhaps at the finish they could draw their house.
- Some children may be able to trace over the numbers with a felt tip pen whilst others might need you to do it for them, but encourage them to watch while you do it.
- Play the game in small groups, helping the children to work out what number the die lands on, then to move that number on the board.

Extensions/variations

- Play dominoes with your children. At first they might have to count the spots but as they gain more experience, they

will be able to instantly recognize one, two or three.
- Encourage the children to look at the pattern that four dots make. Does it look like a square? Do five dots look a bit like a face?

Links to home

- Provide the children with a carrier bag and let them take their family number game home. If possible let them take their die as well in case they do not have one at home. Encourage them to play the game with their parents and their older brothers and sisters as well.

Let's go to market

Learning objectives
- To begin to develop an understanding that numbers are labels
- To begin to recognize coins
- To have an experience of shopping that they might then use in their own play activities

What to do
- Send a letter home to parents, asking for permission to take their child to a shop. You could also ask for volunteers to help you look after the children, a ratio of 1 : 2 adults to children is excellent.
- Use the walk to the market or shop as a real learning experience for the children, pointing out house numbers, shop numbers and numbers on passing buses.
- At the market or green grocer encourage each child to make their purchase talking to them about the prices, the coins that they are using and the change that the green grocer gives.
- When the children get back to your setting, encourage them to describe the journey, talking about what they saw and any numbers that they spotted. How many children bought apples?
- Encourage the children to draw pictures of their trip which you could send to the green grocer as a thank you.

Extension/variation
- Set up a green grocer stall in your role-play area so that the children can re-enact what they did. Use plastic or papier mâché fruit, provide scales, a till and card for the children to write prices on. If you are lucky your green grocer might donate a pack of paper bags for the children to use.

Links to home
- Ask the parents to send in a small amount of money to enable their child to buy some fruit or vegetables. Perhaps they could buy three carrots for their family's tea.

Resources
- Letter home to parents
- Carrier bags to help the children carry their items
- First aid kit
- Find a local green grocer or market which would be prepared to serve a large group of children. Many are more than willing to help, and see it as an excellent learning experience for the children

⚠ Adult supervision is required at a ratio of 1 : 2 adults to children.

This activity involves creating a role-play area that focuses on circle shapes.

• • • • • • • • •

Resources

- Recipe to make pizzas on page 133
- Three-sided screen
- White backing paper
- Poster paints
- Brushes
- Table
- 2 ovens
- Till
- Plastic money
- Telephone
- Plastic pizzas – these can be bought at most toy shops and come with pizza cutters; alternatively, paint thick pieces of cardboard yellow and paint on to the top tomatoes and pieces of pepper
- Ask your local pizza shop if they would be prepared to donate a few take-away boxes and serviettes

Learning objectives

- To show confidence by initiating number activities in a role-play situation
- To think about round or circular shaped objects such as pizzas and wheels
- To be introduced to halves and quarters

What to do

- Gather the children in front of you and ask them to think about round or circular shaped objects. Make a list of them on your easel. Help the children see that a pizza is round and include it in the list,
- Tell them that their role-play area is going to be turned into a pizza parlour.
- Gather a group of willing helpers to set up your pizza parlour.
- Set up your three-sided screen and staple white backing paper on to the walls.
- Help the children paint yellow circles all over the walls.
- Once they are dry, encourage the children to paint a topping on such as tomatoes and pepperoni.
- Set up a table at the front and place on it plastic and cardboard pizzas. Add your take-away boxes, serviettes and pizza cutters.
- At the back of the parlour place two ovens and a table with a telephone so that the children can take telephone orders.

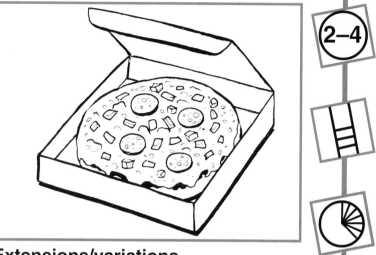

Extensions/variations

- Work alongside the children, asking questions such as *How much is half a pizza?*
- During one of your cooking sessions, help the children to make real pizzas (see page 133 for recipe). You could then have a pizza party.

Links to home

- Encourage the children to find out who in their family likes pizza. Which is the most popular flavour? Is it Hawaiian, vegetarian or meat feast?
- Have the children ever been to a pizza restaurant? How many slices did their pizza have? Did they eat half of it, three-quarters or the whole lot?

2–4

Estimate with cereal

Learning objectives
- To be introduced to the early skills of estimation
- To count up to ten everyday objects
- To begin to develop an understanding of symmetry

What to do
- Put a large bowl of 'chunky' cereal such as Honey Nut Loops in the middle of the table. Ask the children to count out from the bowl ten pieces.
- Then working in pairs encourage one child to put some in their hand and get their friend to estimate how many and then count to see if their guess is right.
- Show the cereal boxes to the children. What shapes can they spot on them?
- How many pieces of cereal do they estimate are in the small box?
- How many do they think might be in the big box?
- Encourage the children to estimate in 'hundreds, tens and units'.
- Encourage them to share their experiences of cereal at home. How many pieces of cereal do their parents eat?

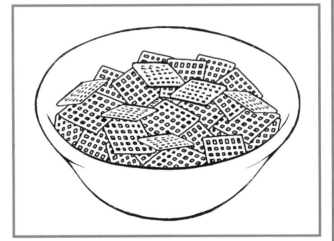

Extension/variation
- Provide the children with a wooden board to work on. Give them a piece of string and ask them to lay it down the middle. Show them how to make symmetrical patterns with the cereal. If they put three in a row on one side of the string, they must do the same on the other. If they put four in a square on one side, they must put four in a square on the other.

Links to home
- Ask the children to estimate the number of items in their food cupboard. Can they estimate how many tea bags are in a box? Most boxes say how many they contain.

Resources
- Breakfast cereals
- Large bowl
- Mini boxes of cereal
- Large boxes of cereal
- Wooden boards
- String

⚠ Be aware that some food items may contain nuts and that some children may have a nut allergy.

The bouncing food cafe

This activity involves creating a café where the food and the staff have to bounce.

• • • • • • • • • •

Resources

- Three-sided screen
- White backing paper
- 4 round tables
- 8 chairs
- Long table
- Notepads
- Aprons
- Pencils
- Till
- Plastic plates
- Plastic cups
- Tissue paper
- Gold plastic baubles for boiled eggs
- Wool for spaghetti
- Green material for lettuce
- Square sponges like scouring pads for sandwiches

Learning objectives

- To show confidence by initiating number activities in a role-play situation
- To handle money
- To role-play café behaviour

What to do

- Gather the children in front of you and ask them to think about what should be in a café.
- Make a list of all the things that they think you need.
- Tell them that this café is going to be a bit different because all the food can bounce, and so can all the waiters and waitresses.
- Set up your three-sided screen and staple white backing paper on to the walls.
- Set up the table and chairs in the café and put a long table at the back where all the food can be laid out.
- Put out a pile of plastic plates and plastic cups with tissue paper inside them to represent drinks.
- Hang up the aprons and place the notepads and the till in the corner for the waiters and waitresses to use.

Extension/variation

- Work alongside the children in their café, developing their vocabulary and helping them initiate number activities. For example, *Table two would like three*

drinks, Table four would like four plates of sandwiches.
The children will love the fact that the food bounces and that they can as well. In the warmer weather, this is a great activity to take outside because then the children can be really energetic.

Links to home

- Encourage the children to talk about games that they play outside at home.
- Encourage parents to give their child the choice of playing indoors or out.

What's your favourite dinner?

Learning objectives

- To record as a group what they find out about food
- To hear mathematical vocabulary. For example *count* and *how many altogether?*
- To recall what they had for dinner yesterday

What to do

- Gather the children into a circle and ask them to think about what they had for dinner yesterday. (Talk about how some people call it *dinner*, some call it *tea* whilst others may call it *supper*.) Some children might find this hard because yesterday seems like a long time ago. However, some might remember. Tell them what you ate for dinner.
- Write down what five of the children had for their dinner.
- On a large piece of card, draw a grid with the meals on the left-hand side and long rows going across to the right-hand side.
- Tell the children that you are going to find out which meal everybody prefers. Ask the children to draw their face on to a sticker and help them stick it alongside their meal choice.
- Gather the children back and encourage them to look at the results. Which is the most popular meal?

Extension/variation

- Give some children clipboards and encourage them to do their own survey about food. Get them to think of two contrasting meals, such as a roast dinner and fish and chips. Have them ask each child which meal they prefer and just make a mark in the appropriate column to record. At the end, ask them to count up their marks and declare which meal is the winner.

Links to home

- Ask the children to find out which are the favourite dinners of each family member. Record the information from each child. Do you have people with the same choices?

Resources

- Large piece of cardboard
- Square white stickers
- Crayons
- Clipboards
  Paper

This activity involves the children being introduced to the idea of heavy and light objects.

•••••••••

Resources

- A variety of heavy objects such as a door stop, a full suitcase, a thick book
- A variety of light objects such as a piece of paper, a feather, a paperclip, a thin book
- 2 hoops
- 2 pieces of card, one labelled **heavy** and the other labelled **light**
- A bunch of bananas
- Multi-link cubes
- Clear balancing scales

Learning objectives

- To use weight vocabulary, for example *heavy*, *light*, *heavier than*, *lighter than*
- To order two objects by weight

What to do

- Sit the children in a circle and place the two hoops in the middle. Place in one the **heavy** sign and in the other the **light** sign.
- Show the children a variety of objects and tell them that today you are going to find out if the objects are heavy or light. Ask them to suggest ways to do this. Help them see that a good way of seeing whether an object is heavy or light is to hold it in your hand.
- Do this for a few objects emphasizing when something is heavy.
- Then get two objects that have not yet gone in the hoop, choose a child, and put one object in each of her hands.
- Show her how to move her hands up and down to decide which object is heavier and which is lighter.
- Beware of some children saying nothing is heavy in order to appear strong!

Extensions/variations

- Present the weighing scales to the children. Put a banana in one pan. Get one child to count as they place cubes in the other

side of the pan. How many cubes make the scales balance?
- Repeat for two bananas. How many cubes make the scales balance? Which is heavier, one banana or two?

Links to home

- Encourage the children to find out if there are any scales in their house.
- What do their parents use them for? Do they weigh ingredients for cooking? Do they weigh themselves on bathroom scales?

Create a garden centre

This activity involves creating a role-play area where your children will love counting flowers and plants.

• • • • • • • • • •

Resources
- Three-sided screen
- White backing paper
- Staple gun
- Stapler
- Poster paints
- Brushes
- Buckets
- Lots of artificial flowers
- Artificial plants
- Large tray
- Small bag of peat
- Plastic flowerpots
- Little table
- Benches
- Plastic cups
- Plastic plates
- Sand timer

Learning objectives
- To show confidence by initiating number activities in a role-play situation
- To use mathematical language when playing

What to do
- Gather the children in front of you and say that you want to change the role-play area into a garden centre.
- Have the children think about what garden centres sell.
- Gather a group of willing helpers and set up the three-sided screen.
- Staple the white paper on to the screen and help the children paint big pictures of flowers on the wall. Can they paint three red flowers? Can they paint three yellow ones?
- Place the buckets and flowers in the garden centre. *How many flowers are there?*, *How many different colours?*
- Fill the tray with peat and place in your garden area. Place the empty flowerpots next to the tray.
- Set up the table and benches for a café area for people to have a drink.

Extensions/variations
- Work alongside the children in the garden centre, asking questions. For example, 'Would it be possible to have ten red

roses, two plants and a drink of orange juice?'
- Ask them to fill the flowerpots with peat. Put a sand timer in the garden centre and ask them, *How long does it take to fill the small pot?*, *How long does it take to fill the big pot?*

Links to home
- Always discourage the children from picking wild flowers when they are out walking. Explain to them that berries are for the birds and not for them.
- Encourage the children to share their experiences of garden centres. What did they see there?

I'm the length of that flower!

This activity involves the children being measured and to realize that they are growing all the time.

• • • • • • • • •

Resources

- String
- Measuring chart posters (available from most bookshops)
- Small pieces of card
- Pencils and crayons
- Scissors
- Blu-tac®
- Thick felt tip pens

Learning objectives

- To put themselves in order by height
- To realize that they are growing just like flowers do
- To use measurement

What to do

- Ask five children to look at each other very closely. Who is the tallest? Who is the shortest? Encourage the children to move themselves around until they think they are in height order.
- Set up a height chart in your setting.
- Work with each child on a one-to-one basis, asking them to stand against the chart, and then cut a piece of string the same length as they are.
- Ask the child to draw a flower on a piece of card and stick it to the length of string. Don't forget to attach a name tag to each flower.
- For some children you may prefer to give them an outline that they colour in and then cut out.
- Blu-tac® the flowers along a wall in your setting with a sign that says, 'Look at our growing flowers'. This should represent the different heights of the children in your setting.

Extensions/variations

- This activity is best done at the beginning of your setting year so that the children can stand next to it and check how much they have grown throughout the year.
- Take every opportunity to talk about height order. Are the children in height order when you have a photograph taken?

Links to home

- Encourage parents to have a measuring chart for their child at home. Encourage them to mark on it once a month, so that the children can observe their growth.

Design a garden out of shapes

This activity involves the children creating the garden of their dreams.

● ● ● ● ● ● ● ● ●

Learning objectives

● To be confident about shape names
● To talk about the shapes that they see and use and about how they are arranged
● To use shape vocabulary, for example *Which shape will fit here?*

What to do

● Talk to the children about the shapes in your garden. Say that today you are going to design a garden using coloured shapes.
● Talk to them about moving the shapes around and only sticking them down when they are happy with their position.
● Encourage them to create a patio using squares, perhaps a flower bed using the rectangles; circles could be flowerpots. What about a pond? Would they have a path running through the garden? Coloured triangles could be used as crazy-paving.
● Ask questions such as: *Which shape could we use for the shed?*, *Which shape would fit in this corner of the garden?* Show the children that by moving the shapes around two triangles can make a square.
● You could display your garden plans in your garden centre.

Extensions/variations

● The children may like to use the same strategy to design a bedroom or lounge.
● Once they have planned it with flat 2D shapes, perhaps they could use 3D junk materials to make a model of it.

Links to home

● Encourage the children to talk about the shapes that they have in their garden. They might have stepping-stone circles going across their grass. Be sympathetic to each child's circumstances. If they do not have their own garden, they could talk about one belonging to a relative or friend.

Resources

■ Sugar paper
■ A variety of coloured sticky shapes such as circles, triangles and squares
■ Glue
■ Junk modelling materials

Gardening

This activity involves the children discussing whose sunflower is the tallest.

• • • • • • • • •

Resources

- Photographs and pictures of sunflowers
- Packets of sunflower seeds
- Magnifying glasses
- Watering cans
- Flowerpots
- Peat
- Compost
- An area where you can store the seedlings that is on the same height as the children
- Camera

Learning objectives

- To use mathematical language, for example *Which is the shortest?, Which is the tallest?*
- To estimate how many sunflower seeds are in a packet

What to do

- This activity is best done in April.
- Ask the children to look at a packet of sunflower seeds. How many do they think are inside?
- Open it up carefully and encourage the children to help you count out the seeds.
- Ask the children to use the magnifying glasses to observe the seeds.
- Show the children how to plant a seed and then allow them to do the same independently.
- Plant a few extras as well, just in case some children's seeds do not grow.
- As the seedlings grow, encourage your children to move them around until they are in height order.

Extensions/variations

- Take photographs of the sunflowers as they progress so that you can have a lasting record. Encourage the children to look at their plants everyday to observe any changes and to decide whether they need water.

2–4

- After several weeks of growth, allow the children to take their seedlings home to plant. Plant your spare ones in your outside area so that the children can continue to observe the growth.

Links to home

- Put a plea out to parents for pots, sunflower seeds and compost. It is better if every child has a sunflower but this means you will need a lot of resources.

Symmetrical flowers

This activity involves the children making bright symmetrical flowers.

• • • • • • • • •

Learning objectives
- To develop an understanding of symmetry
- To create symmetrical flower and butterfly
- To work together to create a number line display and know that the numbers are labels

What to do
- Talk to the children about what symmetry is and remind them about how they made symmetrical patterns with breakfast cereal.
- On your art table show the children how to paint a pattern of a flower on one half of a piece of paper.
- Then quickly fold the piece of paper over.
- Carefully peel the paper open again. You should have the same flower pattern on each side.
- Repeat for the butterfly shape, stressing to the children that they have to be quick painting the pattern.

Extension/variation
- Cut out the children's flowers, add a stem and some leaves. Stick a cardboard number on each flower and staple your flowers to a display board. At first you may want to put up only five, but as your children become more confident you could put up more and make your number line

go up to ten. Mount the butterflies onto sugar paper and display around the flowers.

Links to home
- Encourage parents to point out examples of symmetry in the local environment to their children.

Resources
- Outlines of flower shapes on white paper that has been folded in half
- Outlines of butterfly shapes on white paper that has been folded in half
- Poster paint
- Cardboard numbers
- Display board
- Backing paper
- Sign saying, 'Look at our growing number line'

We care for our garden

This activity involves the children exploring the capacity of water containers.

• • • • • • • • •

Resources
- A variety of water containers
- An outside area
- Some plants and vegetables
- A piece of cardboard
- Thick felt tip pen

Learning objectives
- To order two items by capacity
- To talk mathematically as they take part in normal daily activities

What to do
- Encourage the children to help you care for your outside area by watering the plants.
- Provide them with a variety of water containers such as jugs, buckets, watering cans and saucepans, and ask them to find out which holds the most water and which holds the least.
- The children will have great fun experimenting and will give the plants and vegetables (if you've grown any) a good watering.
- Make a list of all the jobs you think need doing in your garden area, such as tidying the plants of dead heads, watering the plants, checking all the scissors are put back in the correct place.

Extensions/variations
- Give these jobs out on a day-to-day basis. By doing this you will encourage the children to take responsibility for their own environment.
- Make your outside area a priority. It may be that you do fundraising activities to help you buy plants, equipment and suitable surfaces for the children to play

on. All the children could pay to wear green clothes to your setting one day. Alternatively, you could contact local garden centres and DIY stores who may be prepared to donate garden equipment or sponsor you.

Links to home
- Encourage parents to help you make your outside area attractive by having bulb-planting and shrub-planting Saturday mornings. You may have parents who are prepared to donate benches and plant pots.

2–4

Flower arranging

Learning objectives

- To be introduced to length
- To be confident folding a circle into halves and quarters
- To use mathematical vocabulary when doing an art activity

What to do

- Give each child a straw. Let them select a container that they want to use as their vase. Get them to put their straws in straight away so that they can see whether their straws are too tall and will need cutting.
- If you are using white paper art straws, your children should paint them green.
- Once the straws are dry, the children can start making the flower heads. Do this by folding circles of tissue paper in half and then into quarters.
- Tape the points of the shapes they have created to the top of the straw and then carefully open it out and puff it up so that it looks like a flower.
- Using different colours for each flower, repeat until they have a full vase of flowers.
- Help them to cover their vase with a white piece of paper so that they can paint it a bright colour.

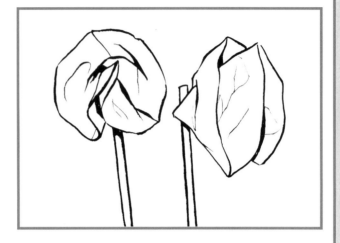

Extensions/variations

- Encourage the children to count how many flowers they have made to go in their vase. *How many red?*, *How many yellow?*
- Encourage the children to think about what else they might fold into halves and quarters, such as clothes or towels. What might they cut into halves and quarters?

Links to home

- This vase of flowers is a great gift idea for Mothering Sunday and looks really pretty.
- Some children may have seen someone cutting the stems of flowers at home because they were too tall for the vase.

Resources

- Art straws or drinking straws
- Large yoghurt pots
- Cylindrical containers that usually contain crisps
- Circles of coloured tissue paper
- Clear sticky tape
- White paper
- Poster paints
- Brushes

© Rebecca Taylor
www.brilliantpublications.co.uk

Combining groups of flowers

This activity will help the children to develop their early addition skills.

• • • • • • • • •

Resources

- 2 hoops
- A variety of artificial flowers
- A soft cat toy

Learning objectives

- To begin to see addition as combining two groups of objects, and subtraction as taking out an object from a group.

What to do

- Gather the children into a circle and place two hoops in the middle.
- Put three flowers in one hoop and two flowers in the other. Encourage the children to work out how many flowers there are altogether.
- Repeat several times with different numbers of flowers.
- If a child feels confident enough, let them put different numbers of flowers into each hoop and then ask the other children to give the answer.
- Now just put one hoop into the middle of the circle. Introduce your naughty pussy cat, who is going to take some of the flowers. Show the children how many he has taken from the hoop and then ask them how many are left. Repeat again with the pussy cat taking different numbers of flowers.

Extensions/variations

- Draw on your easel two cats. Say to the children that you want them to imagine that two cats went into their garden. How many cats' legs would they be able to see in total? How many cats tails?

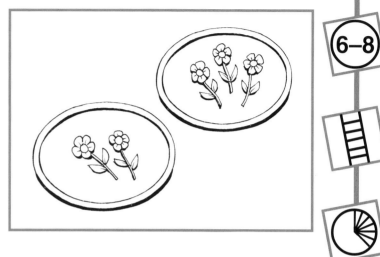

- Draw on your easel two people and a dog. Say to the children that they were looking out into their garden and saw two friends and one dog. How many legs would they be able to see in total?

Links to home

- Encourage the children to try out number problems on their parents at home. For example, *If I had three chocolate bars and you had two, how many would we have altogether?*

Don't forget your toothbrush

Learning objectives
- To tally as a group the colours of their toothbrushes
- To count how many there are of each toothbrush and say one more and one less than that number
- To estimate how many teeth they have

What to do
- Sit the children in a circle, with them each holding their toothbrush on their lap.
- Ask the children to estimate how many toothbrushes there are altogether.
- Have the children estimate how many teeth they have in their mouth.
- Draw up a chart on your easel of the colours that you can see, such as blue, red, green, purple.
- Ask all the children who have blue toothbrushes to come up and put a line in the blue column using a thick felt tip pen.
- Then get all the children to count how many people have blue toothbrushes.
- Once they have worked out the total, encourage the children to say one more than that number and one less.
- Repeat for all the other colours.
- Once you have finished, go over the results with the children. Which is the most popular colour of toothbrush?

Extensions/variations
- Do any of the children have electric tooth-brushes?
- Make sure all members of staff bring in their toothbrush as well.
- It may be that after this session you could invite a dentist to come and talk to the children.

Links to home

> *Dear parents,*
> *At the moment our topic is health and we would be grateful if your child could bring their toothbrush with them tomorrow morning. We are going to be busy counting colours of toothbrushes.*

Resources
- Letter home to parents, requesting the children bring in their toothbrush
- Large white paper to go on your easel
- Thick black felt tip pen
- A dentist who is prepared to give a short talk to the children

© Rebecca Taylor
www.brilliantpublications.co.uk

This activity involves the children learning to enjoy counting while they are taking part in physical exercise.

• • • • • • • • •

Resources
- Sand timers
- Large bikes
- Energetic pop music

Learning objectives
- To compare short periods of time with uniform non-standard units
- To be able to count things they cannot touch

What to do
- This activity can be used on its own or as a quick five-minute warm up with the children before you start any physical activity.
- Ask them to do five jumps on the spot.
- Can they do three star jumps on the spot?
- Can they do ten marches on the spot?
- Can they bend down and reach for their toes four times?
- Turn the sand timer over and ask the children to count how many times they can jump up and down before all the sand runs through.
- Encourage the children to share your large toys outside fairly, using time as a form of measurement. For example, you can ride around the playground on the big bike three times and then you must give the bike to anyone who is waiting for it.

Extensions/variations
- The children really feel a part of it when they have to count, so say to them, *We are going to do three steps forward and then three steps back* or *We are going to lift our knees up five times.*

- Make it even more exciting by doing it to energetic pop music.

Links to home
- Ask the children to count how many stairs they have in their house.
- How many steps do they have in their garden?

It's an obstacle race

Learning objectives

- To use positional vocabulary in a physical context
- To raise heartbeat and develop physical co-ordination
- To take turns

What to do

- It may be that you decide to do this activity as part of your physical education programme. However, you may decide to make it a little bit more exciting and have it as a sponsored event.
- Parents could sponsor the children to go around the course a certain number of times in twenty minutes. Alternatively, you could have it as your main sports day event.
- On the day of the obstacle race, allow the children to help you set up the obstacle course. Talk to them about where you are placing everything.
- Lay everything out, making sure that the children have plenty of opportunities to climb over, crawl through or under a variety of obstacles. Reward the children at the end of the session with a drink and a biscuit.

Extension/variation

- Take photographs of the children doing the obstacle race. Then put them in a big book that the children can look at. Add positional vocabulary sentences under the photographs, such as: *Lauren is crawling under the sheet*, *Ben is behind Thomas on the balancing beam*, *Rebecca is on top of the big stall*.

Links to home

- Let the children take the obstacle race big book home with them so that they can share it with their parents.
- Get them to ask their parents to set up an obstacle course in their garden or at their local park.

Resources

- Large pieces of PE equipment such as stalls and benches
- Beanbags
- Nets
- An old large sheet
- Cones to kick balls around
- Bikes to ride
- Skipping ropes to walk along in a straight line
- Tunnels to crawl through
- Camera, digital or Polaroid
- Large sheets of paper to make big book

⚠ Stress to the children that care should be taken when using the apparatus as we don't want them falling off and hurting themselves.

This activity involves the children having fun doing lots of energetic measuring.

• • • • • • • • • •

Resources

■ Measuring tools such as rulers and tape measures
■ Meter rulers
■ Playground paint

Learning objectives

● To develop estimation skills
● To use a non-arbitrary form of measurement to measure environment

What to do

● In your outside area, encourage the children to estimate how many jumps it will take them to get from one side to the other. Allow them to test it out and see if their estimation was close.

● Show them how to do giant steps. Encourage them to estimate how many they will need to do to get from one end of the playground to the other.

● Show them how to do baby steps. How many of these do they think they will need to do to get across the playground?

● Go inside and repeat the activities but this time perhaps measure your corridor or big play room. Encourage them to tell their findings to their friends, for example *It takes me ten giant steps to get from one end of the corridor to the other.*

Extensions/variations

● If possible, paint a footprint trail in your outside area that the children can follow.

● Have a display of measurement tools such as rulers, meter rulers and tape measures because it is important for the children to know that they exist.

● As well as using their feet to measure show them how they can use their hands as well. How many hand-spans can they measure along a table?

Links to home

● How many baby steps does it take for them to walk the whole length of their garden path? How many giant steps? Can they get their parent to do it? Why is the number now different?

Collecting smiley faces

This involves the children collecting and counting smiley faces for physical activity.

. . . .

Learning objectives

- To count more than ten smiley faces
- To be encouraged to lead an active and healthy lifestyle
- To introduce a scoring system for exercise, for example a swimming trip is worth two smiley faces

What to do

- Gather the children in front of you and encourage them to talk about the physical activities that they do outside of your setting. They could play football down the park, go to swimming lessons, use the trampoline or doing gymnastics.
- Encourage them to think about the physical activities that they do in your setting, such as riding the big bikes, and to join in the games in the hall.
- Show the children the smiley face chart that has their names going down the left-hand side and rows going across to the right, where they are going to collect their smiley faces.
- Talk to them about the scoring system and tell them that the more energy they use the more smiley faces they collect. So swimming might earn them two smiley faces and walking to your setting might earn them only one point.
- Introduce a reward system for everytime the children get ten smiley faces.

Extensions/variations

- Add physical activity pictures to the display chart. Place this at the same height as your children, so they are able to keep counting the faces.
- When the children come in to your setting in the morning and tell you that they have been swimming, immediately reward them by putting the faces on the chart. You may decide to use a similar scoring system to reward good behaviour.

Links to home

- Send a letter home to parents, informing them that you want to introduce a scoring system to encourage a healthy lifestyle. It might also mean that your children ask their parents to walk them to your setting rather than drive.

Resources

- Smiley face stickers
- A large piece of card
- Pictures and photographs of children doing physical activities
- You also need to think about how you are going to reward the children when they collect a certain number of smiley faces. Could they perhaps have an extra five minutes' playtime when they get ten smiley faces?

© Rebecca Taylor
www.brilliantpublications.co.uk

This activity will involve the children getting active for short periods.

• • • • • • • • •

Resources

- A number card for each station
- A plan of your circuit training
- Equipment for your circuit training will depend on what you plan. It could be: benches; hoops; beanbags; balls; cones; sheets
- Sand timer

Learning objectives

- To compare short periods of time with uniform non-standard units
- To raise heartbeats and develop physical co-ordination

What to do

- Plan beforehand how many stations of activity you will include and how many children to have on each one.
- Stations of activity could be: walking along a bench and jumping off; walking a short way with a beanbag on their head; jumping into a hoop and out of it; picking up and throwing a beanbag into a hoop.
- When you start the circuit training, carefully explain what is to be done at each station.
- Allocate a number to each station and explain that the children are going to work for a short time really hard then they are going to stop and have a rest before moving on to the next station.
- Turn the sand timer over and shout 'go'. When all the sand has run through, shout 'stop' and encourage them to sit down for a few minutes before moving on to the next station.

Class

Extension/variation

- After your children have worked so hard, encourage them to wind down by making shapes with their body. For example, they could make letters such as 'X' and 'L'. They could make a curved shape and a straight shape.

Links to home

- Encourage the children to talk about the physical activities that their family does – perhaps their grandma goes to aerobics and their sister plays in a football team.
- Ask them to work together with a partner to create shapes.

Sending and receiving apparatus

Class

This activity involves the children developing their hand – eye co-ordination through ball games.

• • • • • • • • • •

Resources
■ A variety of small apparatus such as beanbags
■ Big soft balls

Learning objectives
● To count the number of times they can send and receive during a physical activity
● To develop hand – eye co-ordination and physical development

What to do
● Provide the children with a variety of apparatus and encourage them to first send and receive independently up into the air.
● Encourage them to do very small throws initially.
● To help them gain confidence, encourage them to pass the apparatus around their bodies, through their legs and round their tummies and backs.
● If children lack confidence, give them a large soft ball because this is easier to catch and if it hits them in the face it will not hurt.
● As the children become more confident, encourage them to work with a friend, perhaps first rolling it to each other, then kicking and then throwing, standing a short distance away from each other.
● Encourage them to count as they send and receive.

Extension/variation
● Encourage all members of staff to work with the children when using the small apparatus. They can partner children who do not feel very confident and also be a good model of how to stand, for example hands ready and watching the ball all the time.

Links to home
● Encourage the children to practise sending and receiving at home with their brothers and sisters and parents. Tell them that practise makes perfect and will help to increase the number of times that they can send and receive without dropping.

This activity involves the children arranging shapes to represent their home.

• • • • • • • • • •

Resources

- A4 sugar paper
- A large number of sticky shapes in a variety of sizes
- Glue
- Black pens

Learning objectives

- To show an interest in shapes
- To show an awareness of similarities in shapes in the environment
- To use appropriate shapes to make a puzzle

What to do

- Gather the children in front of you and encourage them to talk about shapes. What shapes can they see in the room? What shape are the windows? Can they see anything else in the room which is the same shape as the window?
- Provide the children with a piece of sugar paper and a selection of coloured sticky shapes of various sizes.
- Encourage the children to select shapes to make a picture of a house.
- Which shapes could they use to represent the roof? Which shape could they use for the doors? Which shape could they use for the path?
- Encourage the children to arrange their shapes before sticking them down.

Extensions/variations

- During another session, you may ask the children to make a shape person. *Which shape could they use to represent the head?*

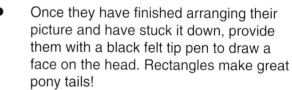

- Once they have finished arranging their picture and have stuck it down, provide them with a black felt tip pen to draw a face on the head. Rectangles make great pony tails!

Links to home

- Encourage parents to ensure that the children have access to lots of puzzles. Making puzzles is a great way to learn about fitting shapes together and can give a lot of satisfaction when they are completed. Many libraries have jigsaws to borrow.

Making a piece of furniture

Learning objectives
- To see how a 3D shape collapses into a net
- To make a piece of furniture that is the right size for a toy
- To manipulate and change 3D shapes

What to do
- Encourage the children to think about all the furniture that they have in their house.
- Tell them that they are going to make a piece of furniture for their favourite small toy.
- Give them many ideas, for example two cereal boxes and four tubes make a great bunk bed, or two cereal boxes and two smaller boxes all fitted together make a great armchair.
- Show the children how if you run your finger along the flaps of a cereal box and open up the ends, you can flatten it out to make a net. You can then rebuild the box, using masking tape along the edges ensuring that the grey side is on the outside making it easier to paint.
- Encourage the children to tell you what they are going to make before they get started.
- Then help them find the appropriate boxes and turn them inside out. Work with the children to help them join their boxes and tubes to make their planned model.

Extension/variation
- Have the children paint their furniture, perhaps with a repeating pattern. They might want to put squares of material on their models for cushions or tablecloths.

Links to home
- Encourage the children to a do a furniture count in their own house. How many chairs do they have? How many tables? How many beds? How many settees?

Resources
- A variety of junk modelling materials: boxes, tubes and yoghurt pots
- Poster paints
- Masking tape
- Toys

House shape game

This activity involves the children experimenting with different shapes.

• • • • • • • • • •

Resources
■ Templates on pages 134 and 135
■ Cord
■ Felt tip pens
■ Clear laminate sheets
■ Scissors
■ Plastic folder with zip
■ Glue

Learning objectives
● To show an interest in shapes
● To name shapes and talk about their properties
● To count up to ten objects
● To take turns

Preparation
● Photocopy on to card six times the template on page 134. Colour with felt tip pens if you want to. Laminate each sheet and then cut out the corresponding shapes that will fit on the base board. Photocopy on to thin card the die, colour in and cover with sticky-back plastic to make it last longer. Store the bits for the game in a plastic folder with a zip.

What to do
● Gather six children together and sit them around a table. Give them each a base board and lay out all the corresponding shapes on the table.
● Encourage the children to throw the die and say what the shape is, collect the correct card and place it on their base board.
● Encourage the children to take turns and not shout out what the die has landed on so that everyone has a fair chance.
● The child who collects all their shapes first is the winner.

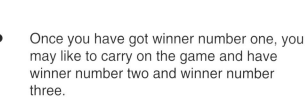

● Once you have got winner number one, you may like to carry on the game and have winner number two and winner number three.

Extension/variation
● Can the children see any symmetry on the house?

Links to home
● Ask the children to find out the answers to the following questions: *How many windows does their house have?, How many doors?, How many rooms?, How many stairs?*

House bingo

Learning objectives
- To recognize the numbers 1–6
- To be able to use a big dice and instantly recognize the one, two and three dots
- To make comments such as *I only have one more to get*

Preparation
- Photocopy on to A3 paper the template on page 136 six times. Allow the children to colour in. Laminate each sheet and then cut out the corresponding shapes that will fit on to the base board.
- Store the bits for the game in a plastic folder with a zip.

What to do
- Gather the children together on the carpet because then you will have more room to throw the die.
- Give them each a game base and lay out all the corresponding number cards on the table. Encourage the children to take it in turns to throw the die say how many dots it has, show the right number of fingers and place the correct card on to their game board.
- The first child to collect all their numbers must shout 'Bingo!' and collects the bingo roof to win the game.

Extension/variation
- Draw a big house on your easel and ask your children to tell you what their house number is. Some children might be able to write the number on the board independently, using a thick felt tip pen.

Links to home
- Ask the children to find out if their parents play bingo.

Resources
- Template on page 136
- A3 paper
- Felt tip pens
- Clear laminate sheets
- Scissors
- Plastic folder with zip
- Large foam die

© Rebecca Taylor
www.brilliantpublications.co.uk

How many body parts?

This activity involves the children counting fingers and toes.

• • • • • • • • • •

Resources
■ Photocopied number line
■ Clear laminate sheets

Learning objectives
● To count up to ten body parts
● To develop estimation skills
● To begin to form numbers and make their mark

What to do
● Gather the children to sit in a circle. Encourage them to count their fingers and thumbs. *How many do they have on each hand?*, *How many do they have altogether?*
● How many fingers do they think there are in the whole room, including everybody?
● Encourage the children to say big number words such as 'hundreds', 'thousands', 'millions'.
● Ask the children to take off their shoes and socks, and look at their toes. How many toes do they have on one foot? How many do they have altogether?
● Ask the children questions such as: *How many legs do you have?*, *How many legs are there altogether when you are looking at two people?*, *How many knees do we have?*, *How many shoulders?*

Extensions/variations
● Have the children draw around their hands with a thick felt tip pen and write down a number in each finger.
● Have the children draw around their feet and write down a number in each toe.

Links to home
● Send home with the children a number line from 1 to 10 that shows the children how to form their numbers correctly. Ask parents to check that their child is forming the numbers correctly as it is hard to get them out of bad habits.

Body bingo

• • • • • • • • •

Learning objectives

6

- To recognize numbers 9–14
- To count dots on a die
- To realize that arranging objects helps counting

Preparation

- Photocopy on to A3 paper, page 137, six times. Colour with felt tips if you want to then laminate each sheet and cut out the corresponding shapes that you will fit on to the game boards. Photocopy on to thin card the die on page 138 and laminate it. Store all the bits for the game in a plastic folder with a zip.

What to do

- Sit the children in groups of six around a table. Give them each a game board and lay all the corresponding number cards out on the table.
- Encourage the children to take turns to throw the die, count the dots and place the right card on to the board.
- Can the children name the shape that they are picking up?
- The first child to collect all their shapes wins the game by shouting 'Body bingo!'

Extension/variation

- Give the children ten beads and show them how to put them into two lines of five to help them count more easily. Give them eight beads, four beads.

Links to home

- You should by now be building a good store of maths games. Your children may borrow books to take home but you might now want to consider whether they can also borrow a maths game to play with their parents. Write a short instruction card to accompany each game.

Resources

- Templates on pages 137 and 138
- A3 paper
- Felt tip pens
- Clear laminate sheets
- Scissors
- Plastic folder with zip
- Glue
- Beads

Mathematical Development

This activity involves the children making a number book about themselves.

• • • • • • • • • •

Resources
- Little books
- Pencils
- Crayons
- Long strips of sugar paper
- Stapler and staples

Learning objectives
- To begin to represent numbers
- To begin to recognize numbers of personal significance
- To use numbers as labels

What to do
- Provide the children with a little blank book and tell them that they are going to make a number book all about themselves.
- On the first page, get them to draw themselves holding a balloon. In the balloon, ask them to write their age. Some children might be able to do this independently whilst others might need to trace over your writing.
- On the next page, get them to draw a picture of their house and write their house number in the middle. You might need to refer to records to check their house number.
- On the third page, you might get them to draw around their foot and then write their shoe size inside it.
- Some children might like to finish by writing page numbers.

Extension/variation
- Make a hat for the children from long strips of paper. Encourage them to write a number on it that is significant to them, such as their age or their house number. Measure the length of paper you need for each child then staple their hat to fit and help the child cut triangles out of the top to make a crown. Have a hat parade in which all the children have to guess why their friend has a particular number on their hat.

Links to home
- Encourage the children to take their book home to share with their parents. Can their parents help them think of any other numbers that are significant to them?

Creating a post office

This activity involves role-playing and scene-setting.

Learning objectives
- To use mathematical language in their play
- To handle money
- To have the confidence to initiate number activities

What to do
- Ask the children to help you make a list of all the things that a post office has.
- Gather a group of willing helpers.
- Set up the three-sided screen. Help the children paint a large picture of a post box on the wall and five brown squares for parcels and ten white squares for letters.
- Set up the tables with one at the front and one at the back. On the front desk place the till, scales and parcels. On the back table set up a working area where the children can wrap parcels, write letters and put them into size order.
- Work alongside the children, taking on the role of a customer and a postal worker. As a customer you may say, for example, *I would like five stamps please*. As a postal worker you may reply, for example, *We only sell stamps in books of six*.

Extensions/variations
- Provide the children with little squares so that they can design their own stamps and stick them on to parcels.
- You may decide to take a trip to your local post office, where the children can all buy their own stamp and post a picture to their parents. The children love to do this and if some children buy first-class stamps and some buy second they can compare when their letters arrive.

Links to home
- Send a letter home asking for permission to take their child to the local post office. This visit will only be possible with volunteers to help you and a donation towards the price of a stamp.
- Have the children ever been to a post office with their parents?

Resources
- 3 sided screen
- Poster paints
- 2 tables
- Till
- Scales
- Used boxes
- Brown paper
- Sticky tape
- Paper
- Envelopes
- Letter home to parents

© Rebecca Taylor
www.brilliantpublications.co.uk

This activity involves the children learning the days of the week.

● ● ● ● ● ● ● ● ●

Resources
- Large piece of card
- Felt tip pen

Learning objectives
● To use the days of the week in conversation
● To count up to ten people
● To appreciate the help of other people

What to do
● Gather the children together and say that today you are going to think about people who help them.
● What have you needed help with this morning? Did you need help to open a door, do up your coat or perhaps make your breakfast?
● Encourage them to help you make a list of all the people who help out in your setting, such as parent helpers, the dustmen, post person, milk delivery person. How many are there?
● Then sing the days of the week with the children. How many days are there?
● Write the days of the week on your easel and then get the children to think about which day people help. For example, you might write that Ben's mum helps on a Wednesday.

Extension/variation
● Throughout the year, the children could help you thank your helpers by making cards and pictures for them. You might decide to do this at Easter and Christmas but also perhaps after this activity because it will really reinforce to the children just how many people help them. How many cards will they need?

Links to home
● Encourage the children to think about all the people who help them at home. They might have a cleaner, a post person, a newspaper delivery person, dustmen, pizza delivery person and gardener!

Making vegetable soup

This activity involves the children making soup, which gives them experience of sharing.

Learning objectives

- To experience measuring in a practical situation
- To experience pouring liquid
- To count in an everyday activity

What to do

- Encourage your children to count your ingredients. How many carrots? How many onions? How many leeks?
- Show the children how to peel and chop the vegetables into small pieces.
- Away from the children, melt the butter in the saucepan and fry the vegetables for 5 minutes, stirring occasionally. Crumble the stock cube into a jug, boil the water in the kettle and pour on to the cube. Stir until dissolved. Add to the vegetables, bring to the boil and simmer for 30 minutes until the vegetables are tender.
- Allow the soup to cool and then tip a small amount into a measuring jug. Allow the children to take turns to pour a small amount through a sieve into another saucepan.
- Add the milk and pepper. Return the soup to heat through.
- Pour the soup into small bowls. How many spoonfuls does each person get? Warn the children to blow on it in case it is hot.
- Encourage the children to talk about how they have all helped each other to make the soup.

- Have a soup party with everyone eating together.

Extension/variation

- You may also to decide to bake bread rolls with the children, which they can eat with their soup. Using a bread mix is very quick and easy.

Links to home

- You may decide to give a copy of the recipe to parents so that the children can try it out at home.
- Encourage the children to cut vegetables into shapes at home. Can they cut carrots into circles? Can they cut potatoes into squares?

Resources

- Small slice of butter, enough to fry the vegetables in
- 4 carrots
- 2 parsnips
- 2 leeks
- 1 onion
- Any other vegetables you decide
- 1 vegetable stock cube
- 600 ml of water
- Kettle
- A pinch of black pepper
- 300 ml semi-skimmed milk
- Measuring jug
- Bowls
- Spoons
- Wooden spoon
- Vegetable parer
- Knife
- Sieve
- 2 saucepans

 Care should be taken when allowing children to peel and chop vegetables.

Mathematical Development

© Rebecca Taylor
www.brilliantpublications.co.uk

Gingerbread men

This activity involves the children learning to appreciate that sometimes things have to be shared out.

• • • • • • • • •

Resources

■ 2 tablespoons clear honey
■ 1 tablespoon golden syrup
■ 25 g of margarine
■ 175 g plain wholemeal flour
■ 1 teaspoon bicarbonate of soda
■ 1 teaspoon cold water
■ 2 teaspoons ground ginger
■ 1 egg yolk
■ Scales
■ Tablespoon
■ Teaspoon
■ Bowl
■ Wooden spoon
■ Saucepan
■ Rolling pin
■ Gingerbread man pastry cutter
■ Large serving plate
■ 2 baking sheets

• • • • • • • • •

⚠ Let the gingerbread men cool before allowing children to share.

Learning objectives

● To measure in a practical situation
● To count during an everyday task
● To face practical problems, for example, *How are we going to share out a gingerbread man?*

What to do

● How are the children going to help each other when they are cooking? Are they going to fasten each other's aprons?
● Spoon the honey and syrup into the saucepan and heat gently with the margarine.
● Put the flour, ground ginger and egg yolk into the bowl and stir in the honey mixture.
● Mix the bicarbonate of soda with the cold water and add to the mixture.
● Encourage the children to take turns to knead the dough on a lightly floured surface until smooth. Roll the dough out thinly and encourage each child to use the pastry cutter to cut out a gingerbread man. Place the gingerbread men on two lightly greased baking trays and cook in the oven for 10 minutes at gas mark 4 or 180°C.
● Allow the gingerbread men to cool and then ask the children to share them out. *Are there enough for everyone? If not, how are you going to share them? Which way should you cut them in half?*

Extension/variation

● Before the children begin to eat their gingerbread man, can they count its body parts? How many arms does it have? How many legs does it have?

Links to home

● Can the children borrow the story of the gingerbread man, available in *Storytelling with Puppets, Props and Playful Tales* (Brilliant Publications) or from their local library? How many characters were chasing the gingerbread man?

The visiting post person

Learning objectives
- To learn that numbers are very important in peoples' jobs
- To learn about numbers in postcodes
- To listen carefully to a visitor

What to do
- Sit the children in a circle and tell them that a special person has arrived who helps many people.
- Ask them how they think a post person helps us. You will find that your children are fascinated by post and love to receive letters through their door.
- How many times in a day do the children see a post person? You might like to explain that there used to be a second delivery but now there is only one.
- Ask the post person to talk to the children, explaining about their job, perhaps the time they get up in the morning and the number of houses they visit.
- Have some children think of questions that they want to ask. For example, *How many times have you been chased by a dog?*, *How many post boxes do you empty?*

Extensions/variations
- After your post person's visit you may like to get the children to tell you what they have learnt. How many things have they remembered?
- Write the children's postcodes on a large piece of card. *How many children's postcodes have a number 3 in them?*, *How many postcodes are there altogether?*

Links to home
- Find out if there are any parents who have connections with your local sorting office who might be able to help you arrange your post person's visit.
- Ask the children to find out what their postcode is.

Resources
- The telephone number of your local sorting office for you to ring to arrange your visit (you will find this in the telephone directory)
- A post person, with trolley and sack if possible
- Large piece of card
- Felt tip pens

This activity involves the children learning that a year consists of four changing seasons.

• • • • • • • • • •

Resources

- Template on page 139, or you could use party plates
- White A4 card for photocopying
- Split pins
- Crayons
- Scissors
- Pictures of seasons such as children playing in the snow, children playing on the beach, a tree with falling leaves and daffodils and lambs

Learning objectives

- To become familiar with the changing seasons, morning and afternoon, day and night
- To begin to know that the seasons are in a cycle and that they keep coming round and every year

Preparation

- Photocopy on to white card the template on page 139 one for each child.
- Cut out the circles and the arrows.

What to do

- Say the season names to the children. Have they heard of them before? What do we do in the summer? What do we do in the winter? Show the season pictures to your children to help stimulate their ideas. How many seasons are there altogether?
- Give each child a wheel, asking them to draw a picture for each season. If it is the summer, you may get the children to draw a large sun. In the next quarter, encourage the children to draw a picture of autumn and so on.
- Push a split pin through the arrow and wheel.

Extension/variation

- You might like to use the template of the wheel to make a day wheel. For example,

in the first quarter the children could draw something they do in the morning, in the second they could draw something they do in the afternoon, in the third quarter something they do in the evening and in the final quarter something they do at night. When they have finished the children can turn the arrow throughout their day.

Links to home

- Encourage parents to help their child focus on a tree that they pass on their way to your setting. What does it look like in winter? What does it look like in spring? Is it covered in blossom and buds?

Making a counting tree

Learning objectives
- To become familiar with the changing seasons and the idea that the environment changes because of the seasons
- To count everyday objects

Preparation
- Find a branch and chisel a hole into a wooden base. Fix the branch into the base to make a changing season tree. Put the tree in your maths area.

What to do
- Talk to the children about what season it is now. What do the trees look like? How could they make the tree in the maths area look like the ones outside? For example, in winter you could make snowflakes out of white paper and stick them on. In spring you could roll up balls of green tissue paper and stick them on to represent blossom. In summer you could stick on green leaves and hang up birds made out of folded fans. In autumn you could make leaves out of orange and brown paper and put pine cones at the bottom.
- Put a sign up next to the tree, encouraging the children to count the objects.

Extension/variation
- Look at the birthday balloons on page 26 that you have displayed in your room. Do the children know what season their birthday is in? If someone has got a

birthday in the winter, what month could it be?

Links to home
- Encourage the children to ask their parents if they could have a small part of their garden to look after throughout the year. For children who do not have a garden they could perhaps have a window box or a pot plant to look after.

Resources
- Branch from a fallen tree
- Wooden circular base for tree
- Coloured tissue paper
- White paper
- Scissors
- Blu-tac®
- Sticky tape
- Green shiny paper
- Assortment of different coloured A4 paper especially orange and brown
- Pine cones

Number igloo

This activity involves the children writing numbers on a winter igloo wall.

• • • • • • • • •

Resources

- Three-sided screen
- White backing paper
- Stapler
- White sheet
- White cushions
- Thick black felt tip pens
- A variety of soft toy penguins and polar bears of different sizes
- A4 card
- Hats
- Gloves
- Scarves

• • • • • • • • •

Please be aware that Polar bears live at the North Pole and Penguins live at the South Pole. They have been grouped together in this activity purely because both regions are cold.

Learning objectives

- To use numbers purposefully in play
- To represent numbers using marks and dots
- To be introduced to addition
- To continue to develop their knowledge of seasons

What to do

- Ask the children to think about which animals like to live in cold, icy environments. Help them to understand that penguins and polar bears are animals who live in cold areas. Encourage the children to think about what season is cold in our country.
- Tell the children that today are going to create a cold, icy igloo for the polar bears and penguins.
- Set up your three-sided screen and cover it with white backing paper. Put white sheets with cushions on the floor, and a box of warm clothing.
- Tell the children that the penguins and polar bears only like eating numbers.
- Can the children write numbers using the felt tip pens on pieces of card and put them in the igloo?
- Encourage the children to dress up for cold weather using the clothes that you have placed in a box in the igloo. Do all the animals have a friend?

Extensions/variations

- Make some simple addition cards, for example 2+1= , 3+1= , 5+1= , and place them in the igloo so that the children can copy them on to the walls and calculate them using the penguins and polar bears.
- Ask the children to put the animals into size order. Which is the biggest penguin?

Links to home

- Ask parents to lend penguins, polar bears and sets of hats and gloves to put inside the igloo for the children to use. Make sure the hats and gloves are clearly labelled.

Teddy bear clock

Learning objectives

- To know about marking specific moments in time. For example, *We all go home at 12 o'clock*
- To form numbers on a clock face
- To develop an idea of the passage of time

Preparation

- Photocopy on to white card the template on page 140. Allow one for each child, for them to colour in later.

What to do

- Show the children a variety of clocks. What time is it at this moment? What time do they have a story? What time do they have their lunch?
- Tell the children that they are going to make a teddy bear clock today.
- Provide the children with some wax crayons and encourage them to decorate their teddy.
- Laminate each if you have time. Cut out the teddy bears and the hands.
- Using a split pin, fix the hands to the middle of the clock.

Extensions/variations

- Sit the children in a circle with their clocks. You may use a teaching clock or alternatively you could make a really big one out of white card and staple this on to the wall with cardboard numbers stuck to

it.

- Make a time on your clock that is significant to the children, for example, *Ten o'clock is drinks time*. Ask them to make the same time on their clock .

Links to home

- Ask the parents to lend different types of clocks, for example alarm clocks, egg timers, travel clocks, wrist watches, sports timers, and make a display of them in your setting.
- Ask the children to count how many clocks they have in their home.

Resources

- Teddy bear clock template on page 140
- White card
- A variety of clocks
- Wax crayons
- Scissors
- Split pins
- Black felt tip pens
- Templates of numbers

⚠ Caution needs to be applied when attaching the split pin.

Sorting seasonal clothes

This activity involves the children sorting clothes for different times of the year.

• • • • • • • • •

Resources

- 4 hoops
- A4 card
- Black felt tip pen
- Plastic sack
- A variety of adult and children's clothes for the different seasons of the year

Learning objectives

- To be able to sort to a set criteria
- To become familiar with ideas such as the changing seasons
- To count everyday objects

What to do

- Gather the children into a circle, ask them to name the four seasons of the year. You could remind them of the time that they made a moving season wheel (see page 85).
- Empty a large sack of children's and adult's clothes which could be worn in different seasons.
- Place two hoops in the middle of the circle. In one hoop, place a sign labelled, 'winter' and in the other the sign 'summer'.
- Go around the circle and ask each child to select an item of clothing from the pile and place it in the appropriate hoop.
- Encourage them to give a reason for their choice. For example, *This woolly hat should go in the winter circle because we need to keep our heads warm when it's cold.*
- Ask the children to help you count how many items of clothing are in each hoop. Do we wear more clothes in the winter?

Extensions/variations

- Add two more hoops to the middle of the circle, labelled 'spring' and 'autumn'.
- Encourage the children to talk about what the weather is like in spring and autumn. For example, in spring the weather starts to get warmer after the winter months and in autumn we are preparing for the winter cold.
- Are there any clothes in the summer hoop that could be moved to the spring hoop? Are there any clothes in the winter hoop that could be moved to the autumn hoop? How many clothes are there now in each hoop?

Links to home

- Encourage parents to involve their children when sorting clothes for holidays and seasons. Can the children fold items in half and quarters? This will really help them when they change for physical activity and need to fold their own clothes.

Class

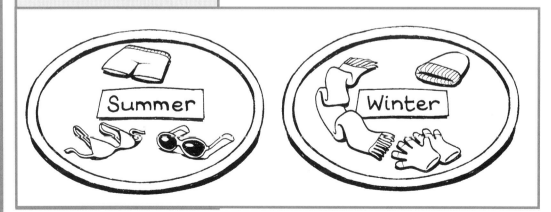

Summer   Winter

Autumn scales

Learning objectives

- To order two items by weight
- To develop the skills of estimation
- To count up to twenty items of nature

What to do

- This activity is best performed in the autumn.
- Tell the children that you need their help to create a nature table. (See Links to home for their contribution.)
- Encourage them to think about what is special about autumn and how we recognize autumn by looking at the natural environment.
- What animals do we see in autumn? Show the children examples of toy animals like squirrels, hedgehogs and foxes.
- Get the children to help you set up the nature table by laying out a green piece of material, adding wicker baskets to put the nature items and the soft toys in, and a pair of bucket scales.
- Show the children how to put an animal in one bucket and then count the conkers into the other bucket until they balance to find out how much the animal weighs. For example, 'Our hedgehog weighs 15 conkers.'

Extensions/variations

- Next, weigh the squirrel using the conkers. *Is the squirrel heavier or lighter than the hedgehog?*

- Encourage the children to find out how many leaves the hedgehog weighs. Why does it take more leaves to balance the hedgehog compared with conkers?
- Have the children put a selection of conkers in their hands and ask a friend to estimate the number of conkers. Have them count together to see if the estimate was correct.

Links to home

- Encourage the children to visit local parks and woods with an adult to collect items of nature. Show them examples of what you would like them to collect, for example pine cones, conkers and leaves. Stress to them that they must never take these from branches but instead look for them after they have fallen.
- Remind the children not to eat the conkers as they are poisonous.

Resources

- Stuffed toy animals, for example a squirrel, hedgehog, fox and badger
- Green material
- Wicker baskets
- Bucket scales
- A variety of natural items collected by the children

⚠ Children should be reminded never to eat conkers or any wild berries as they could be poisonous.

Seaside shop

Seasons

This activity involves the children making a sunny seaside shop, where they can count fishes all day long.

• • • • • • • • •

Resources

- A three-sided screen
- White backing paper
- Paints
- A black felt tip pen
- Sticky white labels
- Stapler
- A variety of items to sell in the seaside shop
- Till
- Plastic money
- Template of a fish
- White paper
- Wax crayons

Learning objectives

- To use numbers purposefully in play
- To join in number songs
- To handle money in a role-play situation
- To create a repeating-pattern fish

What to do

- Ask the children what they think a seaside shop should sell.
- Encourage them to help you set up a seaside shop in your role-play area. Set up a three-sided screen and staple on to it white backing paper. Can the children paint on five fishes? Can they paint on a sun?
- On the front table lay out the items for sale and the till. Provide the children with sticky white labels so that they can price the items.
- Provide the children with two paper outlines of a fish. Ask the children to colour a repeating pattern on each one. Put the two fishes together with the children's colouring on the outside. Place a small amount of newspaper in the middle to stuff them and staple all the way around the edge.
- Place the fishes in the seaside shop with a 1p price on them. How much would five fishes cost?

2–4

Extension/variation

- Use the seaside shop till to solve some fishy problems. For example, *If five fishes cost a total of 5p, which coins could you use to pay for them?*

Links to home

- Ask parents to donate a variety of seaside items that the children could use in their shop. Buckets and spades, shells, sunglasses, hats, windbreaks are good examples.
- Have the children been on any trips to the seaside? What do they think is different? Do they have any photographs they could bring in and show?

Shape collages

• • • • • • • • •

Learning objectives
- To talk about shapes, how they are similar and some are different
- To match simple shapes
- To use size language such as *big* and *little*.

Preparation
- Cut uniform circles, triangles and squares from pieces of sugar paper.

What to do
- Ask the children to find something in your room that is the shape of a circle, triangle and square. Tell the children that today they are going to make shape collages.
- Show them the sticky shapes that they are going to use and talk about how some are big and some are little.
- Provide them with a piece of sugar paper that has been cut into a circle and encourage them to select only circles to stick on to it. Have them stick on both sides of the mobile. Repeat with the triangle and the square. Hole-punch the top of the mobiles, put string through the holes and hang them on your washing line.

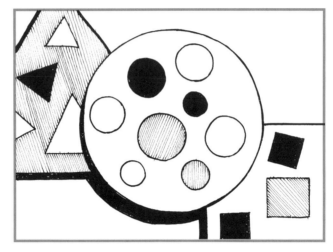

Extension/variation
- Put all your maths jigsaws on a shelf in your maths area that is accessible to your children. Have a particular time in the day when you do jigsaws to help your children recognize shapes and have experience of orientating them. It may be that you always do jigsaws after their snack.

Links to home
- Encourage the children to make a shape collage at home using a wire coat hanger and string. They could cut out of coloured paper squares, triangles, circles, oblongs, hexagons, stars, hearts and diamonds. Their parents could help them cut the string and tie the shapes on to the hanger.

Resources
- Sugar paper
- Templates of shapes
- Scissors
- String
- A variety of sticky circles, squares and triangles all different sizes
- Glue
- Hole punch

© Rebecca Taylor
www.brilliantpublications.co.uk

This activity involves the children discussing the properties of shapes in an exciting game of 'Peepo'.

• • • • • • • • •

Resources

- Cardboard 2D shapes
- Brown envelope or clothes-peg bag
- Plastic or wooden 3D shapes
- Easel
- A4 paper to make a book
- Sticky shapes
- Glue
- Clear sticky tape

Learning objectives

- To use mathematical names for solid 3D shapes and flat 2D shapes
- To learn mathematical terms to describe shapes
- To show curiosity and observation by talking about shapes. For example, *How are they the same?* or *Why are some different?*

What to do

- Show the children your examples of 2D shapes. Can they name them? How many sides do they have? How many corners?
- Ask the children to close their eyes. Put one of the 2D shapes into a big brown envelope. Very slowly, begin to reveal it. Ask the children to guess what the shape is, predicting from what they can see. If a corner is showing it might be a square or a triangle. If no corners are showing it might be a circle. When the whole shape is revealed encourage the children to shout 'Peepo'.
- If a child wants to, you could let them reveal the shapes while you sit with the other children to help them guess.
- Show the children the 3D shapes. What are their names? Behind your easel slowly reveal a part of the 3D shape. Can they predict the shape from what they can see? When the whole shape is revealed encourage the children to shout 'Peepo'.

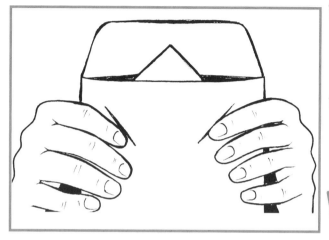

Class

Extension/variation

- Help the children to make their very own 'Lift-the-flap shape book'. Encourage them to stick a sticky shape on to each page and then place a piece of white paper big enough to cover the shape over the top. Fix the paper with a piece of clear sticky tape at the top so that it is a flap. Repeat for all the pages.

Links to home

- Encourage the children to take their books home and share them with their parents. Can they shout 'Peepo' when they reveal the shape?

Shape shop

This activity involves
the children in some
shape shopping.

· · · · · · · · ·

Learning objectives

- To use shape purposefully in play
- To create repeating-pattern shape hats
- To match some shapes by recognizing similarities and orientation

What to do

- Encourage the children to think about what should be in a shape shop. Make sure they include shapes in their suggestions. Encourage them to think about how shapes come in different sizes.
- Set up a three-sided screen, decorate it with big shapes and shape posters that give the children the shape words.
- You might decide to have a 'Shape of the week' poster on the wall with a picture and description of the shape.
- In the shop, set out shape jigsaws, a plastic posting box with 3D shapes and lots of plastic and cardboard 2D shapes that are all different sizes. Put in a box of 3D beads that the children can thread on to string and then sell as necklaces.
- At the back of the shop lay out a working table with sugar paper, sticky paper shapes and glue.

Extension/variation

- Encourage the children to independently make shape collages. On the long strips of sugar paper, show them how to make a

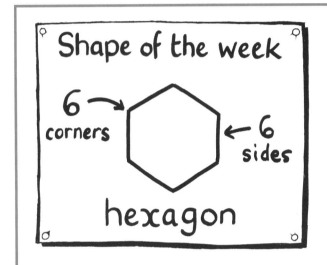

repeating pattern shape hat. At one end they could stick a red circle and then a green triangle, a red circle and a green triangle, and so on. Encourage them to keep going with the pattern until they get right to the end. Measure it around their head and then staple.

Links to home

- Encourage the children to look through an old catalogue at home and cut out anything in the shape of a circle, for example a plate, clock or table. Ask them to stick what they find on a circular piece of paper.

Resources

- Three-sided screen
- 2D and 3D plastic shapes
- Cardboard shapes
- Shape posters
- Shape jigsaws
- Posting box
- 3D beads and string
- Till
- 2 tables
- Sugar paper cut into shapes and long strips
- Coloured sticky shapes
- Glue
- Scissors

Shape swap shop

This activity involves the children swapping shapes.

• • • • • • • • •

Resources
- A variety of cardboard 2D shapes
- Re-usable mastic adhesive

Learning objectives
- To select a named shape
- To match some shapes by recognizing their similarities and orientation
- To co-operate with each other

What to do
- Sit the children in a circle and divide into groups. Place a variety of 2D shapes in the middle.
- Ask one group of children to select a circle from the middle.
- Ask another group to collect squares, another to collect oblongs and another to collect hexagons.
- Ask the children who are holding circles to jump up and down three times. Ask the children who are holding triangles to stretch and touch their toes.
- Ask all the children to stand up and move into the middle of the circle.
- Say that when you shout 'go!' you want them to find somebody else with the same shape and stand with them, holding hands.
- Then ask them to find someone who has a different shape and swap shapes. Everyone shouts, 'swap shop!'

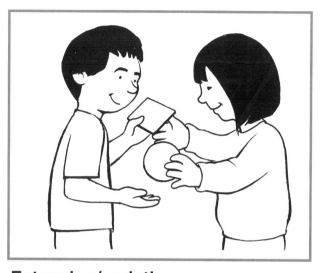

Extension/variation
- Stick the 2D shapes up around the room so that the children can go on a shape hunt. Change the position of the shapes each day so that the children can start hunting all over again.

Links to home
- Ask the children to challenge their brothers and sisters to find certain shaped objects in their home, for example a square tea-bag and a circular cushion.

Let's be robots

• • • • • • • • •

Learning objectives
● To use a remote-control toy
● To give instructions, listen to them and respond with physical actions

What to do
● You will find that nearly all the children in your setting have a programmable toy and will love this activity.
● You may have a selection of remote-control toys or you may need to ask the children to bring in some of their own.
● Sit the children in a circle and place the toys in the middle. Encourage the children to name them and suggest how they work.
● Ask questions to activate a discussion: *What do you have to do to make them work?*, *Do they need batteries to work?*, *Do you have to press an 'on' button?*, *How do you make them move forwards?*, *Do you have to press the arrow?*
● Ask some of the children to programme a toy to get to a certain place in your setting such as the door or wall.
● Tell the children that you are now a robot. Use a robot voice and become very robotic. Ask the children to give you instructions.

Extensions/variations
● Help the children to extend their instructions by using vocabulary such as

two steps forward and *two steps back*, *turn to the right*, *turn to the left*.
● Swap over and let the children be robots. Can they listen to your instructions? Using junk modelling materials help the children make their own robot, cover them with foil and use plastic bottle tops as eyes and nose.

Links to home
● Can the children play robots with their parents? If they had a robot in their house what jobs would they programme it to do? Perhaps tidying their room would be the first job.

Resources
■ A variety of programmable toys such as a remote-control car, boat, dog or robot
■ A variety of boxes and tubes
■ Tubes
■ Plastic bottle tops, foil and paint

Tessellating shape collage

This activity involves the children learning about how some shapes fit together.

• • • • • • • • • •

Resources

- Plastic 2D shapes
- Picture of honeycomb
- Tracing paper
- A large number of hexagons cut out of yellow tissue paper
- Glue
- Circles of yellow felt
- Strips of black felt
- Stuffing
- Needles
- Thread
- Netting
- Bread
- Butter
- Honey

Learning objectives

- To use shape and positional language
- To learn that some shapes tessellate and others do not
- To select a named shape

What to do

- Sit with a small group of children on the carpet and encourage them to play with the plastic 2D shapes. Just by playing with these shapes, they can discover that some fit together but others do not. For example, squares fit together while circles do not. Why do they think that this is the case?
- Show them a picture of a honeycomb and talk about the hexagonal shapes involved. Encourage them to look at it closely and see how all the tiny hexagons tessellate.
- Provide them with a piece of tracing paper and a number of yellow tissue hexagons and encourage them to make their own honeycomb.
- Can they place the hexagons on first before sticking so that they are sure of the position of each shape?
- How many hexagons are in their honeycomb?

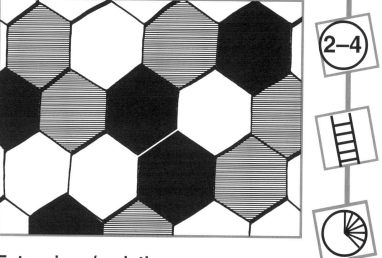

Extensions/variations

- Provide the children with two circles of yellow felt and two strips of black felt. Show them how they can sew around the circle, pull it together and stuff it. Stick on the black strips and perhaps attach some white net for wings.
- Help the children make some honey sandwiches, showing them how to cut them in halves and then into quarters.

Links to home

- Can the children find any examples of tessellating shapes in their home? For example, they may have square kitchen floor tiles that tessellate or hexagonal shaped paving stones on their patio that tessellate.

I spy a shape

Learning objectives
- To use shape vocabulary to name 2D shapes
- To listen to clues and try to predict shapes

What to do
- Gather the children in front of you and tell them that today you are going to play the game 'I spy' with a bit of a difference.
- Say, *I spy with my little eye a shape that is round.* Elicit the answer 'a circle'
- Repeat several times, describing other shapes, and then extend by saying, *I spy a round shape that is in this room.* They might suggest a clock or a round table. You could also introduce the letter that the object begins with.
- Play another game, saying, *I am thinking of a number in my head and it is the number that comes after 3. What number am I thinking of?*
- Ask the children to swap places with you and see if they can lead the game.
- Write the words *I spy* on a piece of card and display in your room.

Extensions/variations
- Using a black felt tip pen draw a different 2D shape on some white stickers.
- Ask one child to stand up and stick a shape on her back.

- Encourage her to walk around the circle so that the other children can see what it is. The other children then have to give clues to help her guess what the shape is, for example 'It has three sides'.

Links to home
- Encourage the children to play 'I spy a shape' with their parents. Perhaps they could do the game in the local park or in their house. How many circles can they spy? How many squares? How many hexagons?

Resources
- White stickers
- Black felt tip pen

This activity involves the children solving problems.

• • • • • • • • •

Resources
■ A variety of soft toys
■ A variety of boxes and containers of different shapes and sizes
■ Model bikes and cars

Learning objectives
● To begin to solve problems
● To begin to view shapes from a different viewpoint
● To respond to silly questions using their shape and size vocabulary

What to do
● Gather the children into a circle and put in the middle a variety of soft toys and boxes and containers.
● Ask the children a silly question, for example, *Will this big toy elephant fit into this little container?* Help the children appreciate that it would not fit. Encourage them to explain the reason. Have them ask each other silly toy questions.
● Encourage them to find a container the teddy will fit into.
● Encourage them to find a container that the doll will fit into. To solve these problems they can decide visually or they could try to put the toy into each box to see if it fits.
● Encourage the children to think about what shapes the toys can see when they are inside the containers.
● Ask the children to imagine they are small enough to walk inside a sweet tube. What shape would they see at the end?

Class

Extension/variation
● Encourage the children to take the toys out to your outside area. Can they select a piece of transport that their toy can travel in? Should the big teddy go on the big bike? Should the little teddy go on the little bike?

Links to home
● Encourage the children to ask their parents fun 'silly shape' questions, for example, *Do you think a dinosaur could get inside this box?*

Repeating-pattern toy

Learning objectives
- To begin to recognize patterns and carry them on
- To look at the shapes of toys and colours

What to do
- Encourage the children to sit in a circle and place a wide variety of toys in the middle of them.
- Place in a line in front of the children a ball, a toy car, followed by another ball and toy car. What do they notice? What would come next in the pattern? Ask a child to carry it on for you. Do this several times and then extend the learning by making a pattern using three toys, such as a ball, a doll and a teddy. What do they notice? What would come next?
- Now encourage the children to make a pattern with the toys using colour. Encourage them to find a red toy and then a blue toy, a red one and then a blue.
- Provide them with a clipboard and ask them to draw the pattern that they have just created. Encourage them to get a friend to carry on the pattern.

Extensions/variations
- Make a fun extension by using the templates on pages 141 and 142. Cut out the shapes from sponge pieces and allow

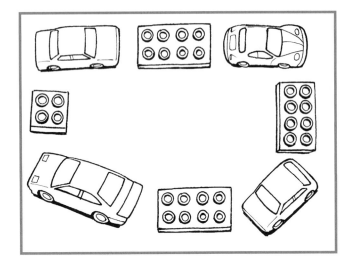

the children to make their own repeating patterns using the sponges and different coloured paints.
- The templates can also be used to make paper cut-outs on coloured sticky paper. Give the children a long strip of sugar paper and let them stick on a repeating-pattern using the toy shapes.

Links to home
- Encourage the children to make repeating patterns with their toys at home. Can they make patterns with other things at home, such as kitchen equipment? For example, spoon, fork, spoon, fork?

Resources
- A variety of toys, all shapes and colours
- Strips of sugar paper
- Coloured sticky paper
- Toy templates on pages 141 and 142
- Sponges
- Paints

Teddy bear paper chain

This activity involves the children cutting out a chain of teddies.

Resources
- Long strips of sugar paper
- Teddy template on page 143
- Scissors
- Pencils
- Wax crayons
- Roll of white wallpaper to create large bear chain

⚠ Adult supervision is needed when the children are using scissors.

Learning objectives
- To begin to develop knowledge of symmetry
- To develop cutting-out skills
- To practise the formation of numbers

What to do
- Show the children a long strip of sugar paper and get them to watch you folding it into a concertina.
- On the top piece of paper, show them how to draw around the teddy template on page 143 making sure that the arms and the feet touch the edges.
- Show them how to hold all the paper together and then cut around the shape.
- Carefully help them to reveal all the teddy bears. Where is the line of symmetry?
- Can they now write a number on each bear? Some children may need to trace over your numbers.
- Can they draw eyes, a nose and a mouth on each bear?
- Can they colour the bears in a repeating pattern with wax crayons?

Extension/variation
- You could make large teddy bear chains using a roll of white wall paper. Ask the children to paint them and then put them on the wall as a number line. At Easter time you could do a number line of eggs or Easter bunnies and at Christmas a number line of Christmas trees or presents.

Links to home
- Can the children show their parents how to make a teddy bear chain? Can they experiment and produce a chain of cars or trains instead?

Our tiger keeps eating numbers!

• • • • • • • • •

Learning objectives
- To use knowledge of the order of numbers to identify the missing numbers
- To compare two numbers and use language such as *more than* and *less than*
- To find one more or one less than a number from 1 to 10

What to do
- Introduce your tiger to the children (see page 15).
- Say that today your tiger is very hungry and he has just whispered to you that he really likes eating numbers.
- Show the children your large number cards. Can they say the numbers that they see?
- Say that you are going to give one of the cards to the tiger and then they are going to look at the other cards that are left and decide which one is missing.
- Give a card face down to the tiger so that the children cannot see which one it is. Then lay out all the cards face up and see if the children can identify which one is missing.
- Encourage the children to explain how they worked out which number the tiger had eaten.

Extensions/variations
- Show the children a number and explain that you are going to ask the tiger to say what the following number is. Make the

tiger say the wrong number so that the children have to shout out to correct him. Repeat several times.
- Put two numbers up on your easel and get the tiger to point to the number which is greater or smaller, saying: *Which number is more than, or less than, this one?* Encourage the children to think about whether the tiger is right.

Links to home
- Provide the children with a set of white cards numbered 1–10 to take home. Write down some activities that the children can do with their parents, such as putting them in the right order or hiding one and trying to guess which one is missing.

Resources
- Your toy tiger (preferably with mouth that opens)
- Large number cards
- White cards numbered 1–10

Setting up a toy shop

This activity involves the children setting up a toy shop and making price labels.

• • • • • • • • • •

Resources

- A variety of toys
- 2 tables
- Till
- Chairs
- Paper carrier bags
- Telephone
- A4 card
- Sticky white labels
- Large felt tip pens
- Camera

• • • • • • • • • •

 Use paper carrier bags to avoid the danger of suffocation.

Learning objectives

- To use numbers in role-play activities
- To handle money and make price labels
- To use shop vocabulary such as *sale*, *receipt*, *change*

What to do

- You may have a selection of toys or you may like to ask the children to bring in some toys to help you set up your toy shop.
- Get the children to help you lay out the toys on the tables. Encourage the children to sort them. Should all the soft toys be on one table and all the other toys on the other?
- Help them set up the till and the carrier bags and the telephone.
- On A4 card write some signs to go in the shop such as *SALE; Would you like a carrier bag? Please ask if you can't find the toy that you require*.
- Encourage the children to use the white sticky labels and the thick felt tip pens and price the toys themselves. Ask them questions, for example, *How much is the teddy?*, *Is the ball more expensive than the car?*

Extensions/variations

- Take photographs of the children working in the toy shop. Display them – parents will find them interesting and the children will love to look at them.

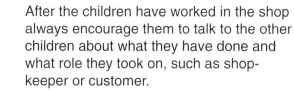

- After the children have worked in the shop always encourage them to talk to the other children about what they have done and what role they took on, such as shop-keeper or customer.

Links to home

- You may like your children to find out what toys their parents used to play with when they were little. If the parents still have the toys, how old are they now? How old are the children's toys?

Hide and seek

• • • • • • • •

Learning objectives

- To use positional vocabulary and give each other directions
- To measure time with an egg timer
- To make dens outside for their toys

What to do

- Tell the children that you have hidden a teddy in the room and that you want them to find it. Say that you will give clues to the children such as 'move forward', 'move to your left' or 'move to your right' and 'reach up high'.
- Encourage them to hide a toy and then give instructions to their friends on how to find it without giving away its location immediately.
- Talk to the children about how you can also say 'warm' and 'hot' as someone gets close to the hidden toy or 'cold' and 'freezing' as they move away.
- Encourage the children to make exciting dens for toys in your outside area. Hide a toy inside one and using a stopwatch or an egg timer see how long it takes the children to find it.

Extensions/variations

- Hide some plastic and wooden numbers in your sand tray.
- How many numbers can the children find? Once the children have found them all, can they put them all in the right order?

Links to home

- Can they play the same hide and seek game with their brothers and sisters at home?

Resources

- A variety of toys
- Cardboard boxes
- Large sheets of material to make dens
- Stop watch or egg timer
- Plastic numbers
- Wooden numbers

Creating a travel agents

This activity involves the children booking holidays and working out how long it will take to get there.

● ● ● ● ● ● ● ●

Resources

- A variety of travel brochures
- Guide books
- Maps
- Two tables
- Old suitcase
- A variety of summer clothes
- Old computer key board
- Foreign currency

Learning objectives

- To begin to develop an understanding of the time it takes to travel to a foreign country
- To be introduced to foreign currency. How is it different from our money? Talk about the euro and the countries involved

What to do

- This activity is best done in the summer term when perhaps the children are looking forward to their summer holidays.
- Get the children to help you set up the travel agent's. Spread holiday brochures, guide books and maps over a table.
- Then set up a desk that has the computer keyboard where the travel agent can check for availability.
- Place the suitcase in the corner with all the summer clothes, where the children can go and start packing for their holidays.
- Work alongside the children, asking questions such as *I would like to go on holiday to New Zealand. How long is the flight time?*

Extensions/variations

- Encourage the children to think about which is the quickest form of transport. How long did it take them to reach their last holiday destination?
- Show the children a variety of foreign currencies. How are they different from our money? Are the colours different and are the coins smaller?

Links to home

- Ask parents to lend you guide books, maps and travel brochures and old suitcases if they have any.

Our car park

Learning objectives

(2–4)

- To develop counting skills
- To begin to develop an appreciation of the importance of numbers when organizing toys and belongings

Preparation

- In your outside area, using special play-ground paint, paint a road for your children to ride their vehicles along. In a suitable position mark out a car park with enough spaces for the vehicles you have. Paint a number on each vehicle and put a corresponding number in each parking space.

What to do

- Provide your children with regular opportunities to play outside on the marked-out road and car park.
- Encourage the children to think about which number space they should park their car in.
- You might decide to shout 'car park' as a signal for the children to park their cars in the correct spaces.

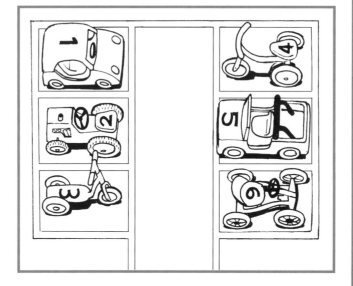

Extensions/variations

- Looking out of your setting window, encourage your children to do a survey of all the different coloured cars that go past.
- If the children's parents have a car, what colour is it? Do a survey to find out which is the most popular colour for a car.

Links to home

- Have the children been in a multistorey car park? How many floors did it have? How many spaces? How much did it cost to park there?

This activity involves the children realizing the importance of numbers when they are organizing the car park.

• • • • • • • • •

Resources

- Cars
- Bikes
- Playground paint
- Outside area

Bus role play

This activity will involve the children solving problems. Are there enough seats for every passenger?

• • • • • • • • •

Resources

- Plastic box with money
- Bus driver's hat and others hats and bags inside for other passengers to use
- Chairs
- Boxes
- Round tray for steering wheel

Learning objectives

- To solve practical problems
- To involve number-solving and use number vocabulary in play

What to do

- You may decide not to have this as a fixed role-play area but instead have a box with all your props in that the children can go to whenever they want to set up a bus. By doing this the children will have an opportunity to arrange the seating plan.
- Encourage them to think about how the seats are arranged on a bus.
- Have they noticed there is always a central aisle?
- If more children join the activity, encourage the children to work out where they are going to sit if all the places are filled. Should some children get off or should more seats be collected and the bus made longer?
- Encourage the driver to collect the money and drive. The children may also like to sing while travelling, for example 'The wheels on the bus go round and round ... '.

Extension/variation

- Have the children think about how they could change the bus. What other transport could it become? If it became a train, what changes would they need to

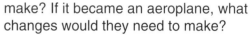

make? If it became an aeroplane, what changes would they need to make?

Links to home

- Encourage the children to talk about their own experiences of buses. Have they got any bus or train tickets at home that they could bring in to show and use on 'our bus'?

How many wheels

This activity helps the children to develop early addition skills.

● ● ● ● ● ● ● ● ●

Resources
- Whiteboards
- Wipeable pens

Learning objectives
- To develop counting skills
- To use the vocabulary involved in adding and subtracting
- To begin to relate addition to combining two groups of objects

What to do
- Sit the children in a circle and give them each a whiteboard and a wipeable pen.
- Draw a bike on your easel and ask them to do the same on their whiteboards and then count how many wheels it has.
- Encourage them to repeat for two bikes and then three bikes.
- Draw a car on the board and ask how many wheels it has.
- Ask them why they cannot see four wheels on your picture. Explain that the other two are on the other side of the car and you cannot see them from this side. Can they draw two cars? Can they tell you how many wheels there are in total?
- Ask them to think about how many wheels a tricycle has, how many wheels a big lorry has. Why do they think a big lorry has more wheels and what do they notice about the size of lorry wheels?

Extension/variation
- Ask the children to draw two bikes again. Tell them a little boy has just come along and taken one of the wheels off one of the bikes. Rub it out and then ask them to tell you how many wheels are left. Repeat with different numbers of bikes.

Links to home
- Encourage parents to read to your children every day if possible. Suggest that they ask maths questions about the book as well as literacy ones, for example, 'How many pigs are in the story?'

How far will my car travel?

This activity involves the children sending cars down a ramp.

• • • • • • • • • •

Resources
- A variety of toy cars
- A wooden plank
- A variety of thick books
- A variety of floor coverings such as a bumpy mat, a piece of plastic
- A selection of equipment to measure such as pencils

Learning objectives
- To use non-arbitrary measurement
- To experience measuring length
- To discover if the height of the ramp affects how far the car travels

What to do
- Help the children to set up a plank that leans against five thick books and slopes down on to a large carpet space.
- Allow a small group to queue up with their cars and then take it in turns to roll their car down the ramp.
- Once the cars have rolled down the ramp, how far have they travelled? Whose car went the furthest?
- Ask the children how they think they could measure the distance that the cars travel. Some might suggest measuring from the bottom of the plank to where the car stopped with pencils, baby footsteps or giant footsteps. Some children may suggest using a ruler.
- Repeat the exercise again and this time get everyone to help measuring the distance travelled using the same non-arbitrary form of measurement.

Extensions/variations
- Extend the activity by getting the children to raise the height of the ramp with more books underneath it. See if that affects the distance the car travels.
- Change the surface under the ramp to see if that affects the distance the car travels. For example, place a piece of plastic underneath it or a bumpy mat.

How many cups?

This activity involves the children finding out how many cups fill a jug.

● ● ● ● ● ● ● ● ●

Learning objectives
● To solve practical everyday problems
● To put containers into order by capacity
● To use vocabulary such as *This container holds more than that one*

What to do
● Gather a group around the water tray and ask them to select two containers and one cup.
● Tell them that they are going to find out which container holds more by counting how many cups they can pour into each one.
● Fill a cup up and show how it is full. Explain that every cup that they pour in must be full otherwise it will not be fair.
● Help the children find out how many cups it takes to fill each container and then decide which container holds more.
● Extend the learning by encouraging the children to order three containers.
● Sometimes the shape of a container can mislead you about the quantity it holds and it is good for the children to discover this.
● Older children could stick a sticky label on to containers, saying the number of cups they hold.

Extensions/variations
● In the summer, encourage your children to have tea parties for their toys outside. Help them to fill a plastic teapot with water and then find out how many cups it will fill.
● Ensure a plentiful supply of water is available to the children during the summer. Allow them to pour water into cups for everyone.

Links to home
● Ask parents to donate plastic bottles and containers for this activity. Remember glass bottles are not suitable in case they crack or smash.

Resources
■ Water tray
■ Water
■ Plastic containers
■ Cups
■ Stick labels
■ Plastic teapots

Full, half full, empty

This activity introduces the children to the vocabulary of capacity.

• • • • • • • • •

Resources
- A large numbers of plastic containers
- Water and water tray
- Food colouring
- A4 card
- Felt tip pens
- Sand and sand tray

Learning objectives
- To use capacity vocabulary
- To be introduced to measurement
- To use capacity in play

What to do
- This activity is best done in the summer when you can take your water tray outside and let the children really enjoy experimenting. Adding food colouring to the water will also help to grab their attention and make the activity fun.
- Gather a group of children around the water tray and say that you are going to show them some different things that you can do with water and a container.
- First, show the container to the children and ask them how they would describe it when the container has got nothing in it. Encourage them to say that it is empty.
- Then show the children how to make the container full and half-full. You can say 'half-empty' but 'half-full' is much more positive.
- Finally, show the children how you can make the container overflow.

Extensions/variations
- Encourage the children to have a go in the water tray by themselves, experimenting with different sized containers.
- Remember that capacity is all about dried goods as well, so the children can use the same vocabulary in the sand tray.
- Display the words with a visual picture to help the children.

Links to home
- Encourage your children to show their parents what they have learnt at bath time, when washing up and perhaps in their paddling pool during the summer months.

www.brilliantpublications.co.uk

Ice sculpture

Learning objectives
- To find out how many cups of water it takes to fill a washing-up glove and balloon
- To observe how long it takes for ice sculpture to melt

What to do
- Show the children your washing-up glove and get them to count how many cups of water it takes to fill it up.
- Peg it and hang it in the freezer.
- Encourage them to think about what will happen to it in the freezer.
- How long do they think it will take to freeze? It usually takes about a day and a night.
- Repeat the same process for the balloon, but tie a knot in it instead.
- Once the sculptures are ready, take them out of the freezer and place them in a tray. Cut away the glove and balloon and allow the children to observe the sculptures and touch the hard frozen ice.
- Encourage the children to observe how long it takes for the sculptures to melt.

Extension/variation
- Add food colouring to the water you put inside the washing-up glove to make the sculpture even more exciting.

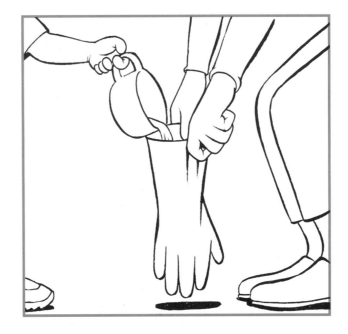

Links to home
- Encourage the children to talk about their experiences of ice at home. They might have it in drinks in the summer or they might have had an ice pack put on their head.

Resources
- Large rubber washing-up gloves
- Balloons
- Small cup
- Food colouring

Water race

This activity involves the children having a race carrying cups of water.

● ● ● ● ● ● ● ●

Resources
■ Two plastic buckets
■ Cups
■ Plastic tennis bat
■ Hoops
■ Beanbags
■ Football
■ Camera/video camera
■ Stop watch or watch with second hand

● ● ● ● ● ● ● ●

⚠ It might be appropriate for children to wear plimsolls when they participate in this activity.

Learning objectives
● To use capacity vocabulary such as *full*
● To count how many cups their team can travel with
● To begin to develop an understanding of how time is used in races

What to do
● This is a great activity to do on your sports day.
● Put the children into teams.
● Place a bucket of water with a team of children and a plastic tennis bat and a plastic cup. A little distance away place an empty bucket and the rest of the children, who are going to count how many cups they see poured into the bucket.
● Tell the team that you are going to start your watch and then see how many cups of water they can get into the bucket in three minutes.
● Show the first child how to fill their cup, balance it on the bat and then walk to the empty bucket and empty it. They then have to run all the way back to their team before the next member can have a go.
● At the end of the three minutes ask the other children to declare how many cups were poured into the bucket.

Extension/variation
● Allow other teams to have a go and then try out other races. For example, how many beanbags can the team throw into a hoop in three minutes? How many times can the team kick a ball into goal in three minutes?

Links to home
● Invite all parents to your sports day. For parents who cannot make it, take lots of photos and perhaps even video it. You can then sell the photo's and/or video to parents for a small charge.

Daily weather chart

This activity encourages the children to become weather people just like on the television.

Learning objectives
- To learn the days of the week and months of the year
- To begin to use time vocabulary such as *today* and *yesterday*
- To make daily weather observations

What to do
- Make this activity as part of your everyday routine.
- Sit the children in front of you and ask them the following questions:
    - What day is it today?
    - What day was is it yesterday?
    - What day is it tomorrow?
    - Do you know today's date?

  Write all their responses up on your easel.
- Photocopy and cut out the weather symbols on page 144. Ask the children to describe today's weather. Take turns for children to choose a weather symbol and stick it onto your chart.
- By doing this activity every day the children will become confident of the days of the week and you will find that they ask their parents in the morning what day it is so that they can answer your questions.

Extension/variation
- Talk to the children about weather forecasters. You might get the children to draw some weather scenes and then send them off to your local television centre.

Monday	☀
Tuesday	☀ ☁
Wednesday	☁🌧
Thursday	☁🌧
Friday	☀

Links to home
- Ask the children to find out if they have a barometer in their home. How does it tell us what the weather is going to be like? Do they watch weather forecasts with their parents?

Resources
- Template from page 144
  Easel
- Pen for writing on easel
- Paper and drawing implements

This activity involves the children collecting rainwater in a exciting way.

Resources

- Clear plastic water bottles
- Sharp scissors
- An outside area to place your funnels in
- Permanent marker

⚠ Remind the children that they should not drink rainwater as it could contain pollutants.

Learning objectives

- To use capacity in an everyday situation
- To use capacity vocabulary
- To use non-arbitrary measurement

Preparation

- Take a clear water bottle and cut it in half. Discard the bottom of the bottle and keep the top part with the bottle top on to be your rain collector. Do this to several bottles.

What to do

- Show the children the bottle collector and explain that you are going to pour a cup of water into it and mark the level of the water with your permanent marker. This will mean that when the rain reaches this line a whole cup of rain has been collected.
- Repeat this process for two cups and three cups.
- Go outside with the children and ask them where they think the rain collectors should go. Dig a hole and push them in. Wait for rain.

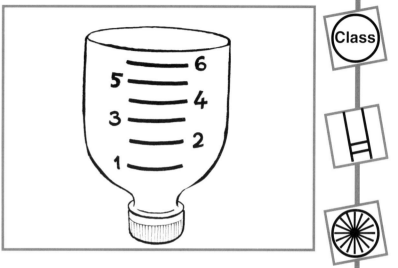

Extensions/variations

- You might decide to get the children to record each day how much water has been collected. For example, 'On Monday one cup was collected.'
- At the end of the month, encourage the children to think about whether it has been a wet or dry month.

Links to home

- Encourage the children to find out if they collect water at home.
- How can they help their parents to save water? For example, sharing bath water.

Make a kite

• • • • • • • • •

Learning objectives

- To make an object that is in the shape of a diamond
- To change the shape slightly in order to attach sticks and string and make it into a kite

Preparation

- On the large piece of card, draw a template of a large diamond. Place this on to your tissue paper and cut out a diamond shape for each child. Collect your resources together and gather the children together.

What to do

- Ask the children to talk about the shape you have cut out and what they think could be made from these items.
- Show them how to place two sticks in a cross shape and bind string around the middle.
- Tape the sticks on to the diamond tissue paper at each point of the diamond.
- Tie a very long piece of string on to the middle of the cross and show the children how to wind it around the kitchen roll tube.
- Add a tail at one end of the kite made from a long thin piece of tissue paper.

Extensions/variations

- Using other shapes and sticky paper help the children to make a face for their kite and stick it on to the tissue paper. You may need to tape over the top of the shapes to ensure that they do not come off.
- Wait for a windy day when the children can take their kites into the outside area and run with them.

Links to home

- Encourage the children to talk about whether they have a kite at home and what shape it is. Where do they fly their kite and what does the weather have to be like?

Resources

- A large piece of card
- Large sheets of tissue paper
- Green garden sticks
- A big ball of string
- Kitchen roll tubes
- Clear sticky tape
- Glue
- Coloured sticky paper

© Rebecca Taylor
www.brilliantpublications.co.uk

This activity involves the children being introduced to simple data handling.

• • • • • • • •

Resources

- ■ Large piece of card
- ■ Sticky fasteners
- ■ Template on page 144
- ■ Black felt pen

Learning objectives

- ● To be introduced to early data handling
- ● To work together to create a group chart
- ● To answer simple questions about the chart

What to do

- ● Ask the children to think about the type of weather they really enjoy. Say that today they are going to make a chart which will show the most popular type of weather.
- ● Talk to them about symbols of weather. If they like hot weather they could use the sun symbol. If they like rain, they could use the cloud with rain drops coming out of it. If they like snow, they could use the snowman symbol.
- ● In front of them, draw an axis on the large piece of card with the types of weather along the horizontal axis and the number of children up the vertical axis.
- ● Using the template on page 136, photo-copy the symbols on to thin card, cut out and put a sticky fastener on the back.
- ● Ask the children to pick a symbol that describes the weather they like best and stick it on the chart.

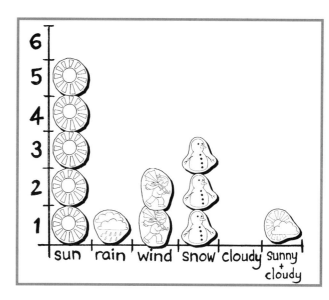

Extension/variation

- ● Once the graph is complete, encourage the children to draw some conclusions from the information. How many children like hot weather? How many like the snow? How many like the rain? Which is the most popular type of weather? Which is the least popular?

Links to home

- ● Ask the children to find out what their parents' favourite type of weather is, and perhaps what their favourite month is and why.

Bear washing line

Photocopy the bear 10 times and cut it out. Write a number from 1–10 in the centre of each bear's tummy and let the children colour in.

Ten brown bears

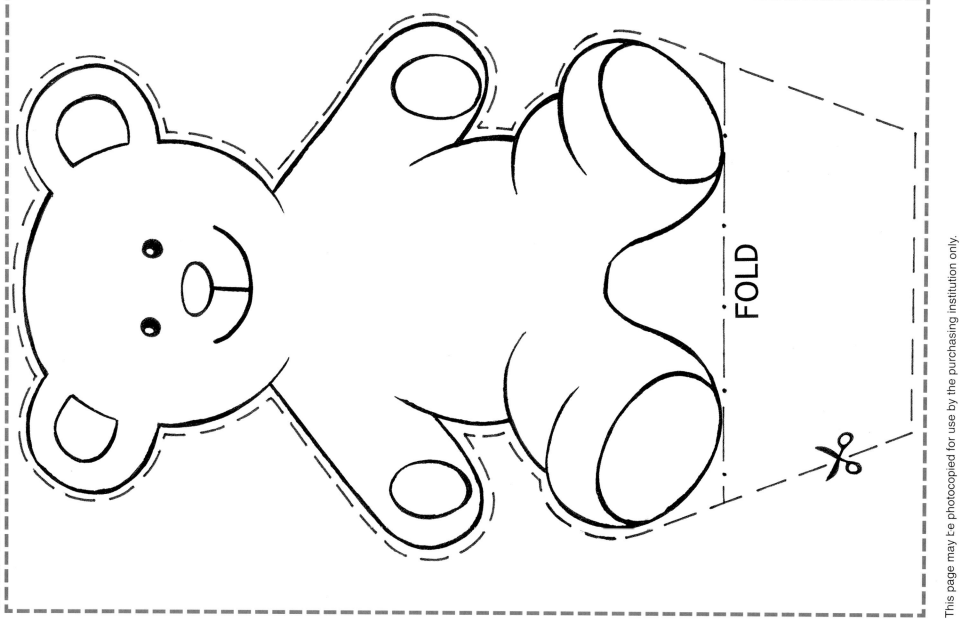

FOLD

Photocopy the bear ten times. Let the children colour them in. Cut out bears and old along dotted line and slide tab into slits in box.

This page may be photocopied for use by the purchasing institution only.

© Rebecca Taylor
www.brilliantpublications.co.uk

It's my birthday today!

It's my birthday today!

Today is a special day for

Birthday child to colour in. Attach ribbon to badge and let the child wear it for their special day.

Countdown to Christmas

Photocopy the snowmen or encourage the children to draw their own. Glue onto backs of old Christmas cards.

This page may be photocopied for use by the purchasing institution only.

Christmas shop

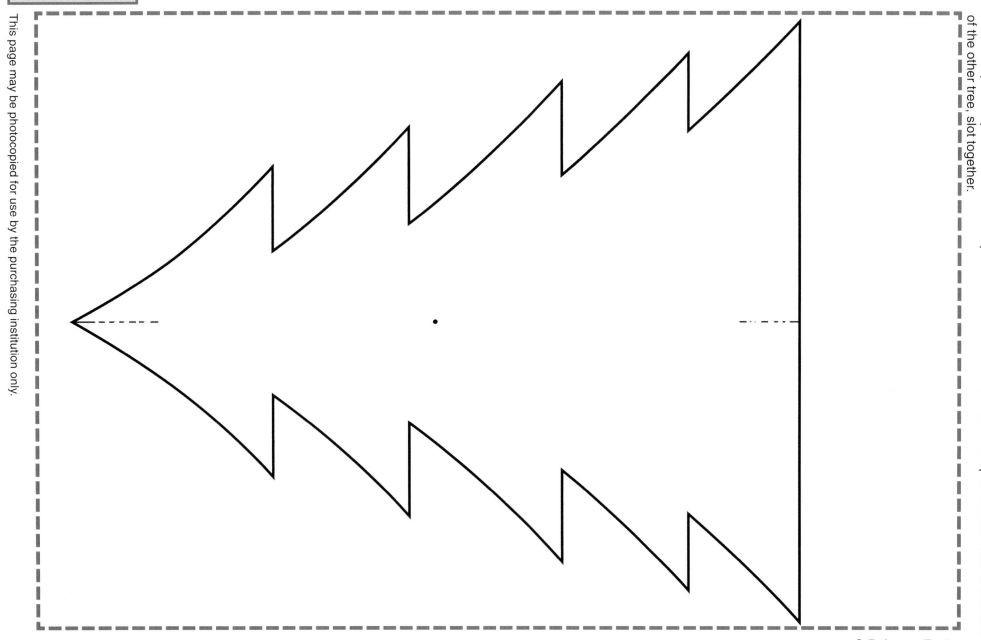

Make two photocopies for each tree required. Colour and decorate. Slit the top of one tree and the bottom of the other tree, slot together.

Mathematical Development

Chinese New Year – ideas

Chinese lanterns

Follow the instructions step by step to make your Chinese lantern.

Step 1

Give the children a piece of A4 paper and ask them to colour it in brightly.

Fold paper in half and cut up from folded edge with scissors to approximately halfway in.

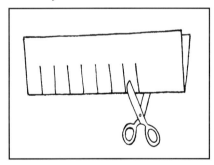

Step 2

Open out paper carefully.

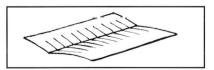

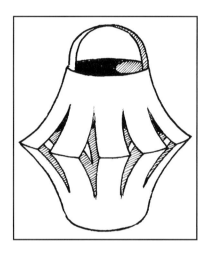

Step 3

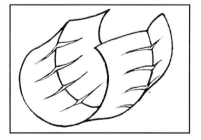

Bring short sides together and glue. Press top towards the bottom and glue on a handle.

Fortune cookies

Inside each little folded biscuit is a slip of paper with a message on it. You can have great fun thinking up what to write. Usually the fortunes are such things as: 'Beware of a tall stranger', or 'You are lucky today!'.

Ingredients

2 eggs; 50 g (2 oz) sugar; a pinch of salt; 50 g (2 oz) butter; 50 g (2 oz) plain flour; a few drops of vanilla essence.

Step 1

Set the oven temperature at 180°C (350°F), or gas mark 4. Write out your fortunes on 12 strips of thin paper about 6 x 1 cm in size.

Step 2

Carefully break each egg in half over a medium sized bowl. Pass the egg from one half of the shell to the other, letting the white of the egg fall into the bowl. Put the yolks to one side as you don't need them for this recipe.

Step 3

Stir the sugar into the egg whites and add the salt. Mix well. Melt the butter in a small saucepan and pour it into the whites. Add the flour and vanilla and beat well until smooth.

Step 4

Drop the batter, 1 teaspoon at a time on to a greased baking tray, making sure that the cookies are at least 5 cm apart.

Step 5

Place in the oven for 5 minutes or until the edges are brown.

Step 6

Wearing oven gloves, take the tray out of the oven. Place a fortune in the middle of each cookie and fold into quarters using a palette knife. This has to be done while the cookies are still hot.

Chinese New Year dragon face mask

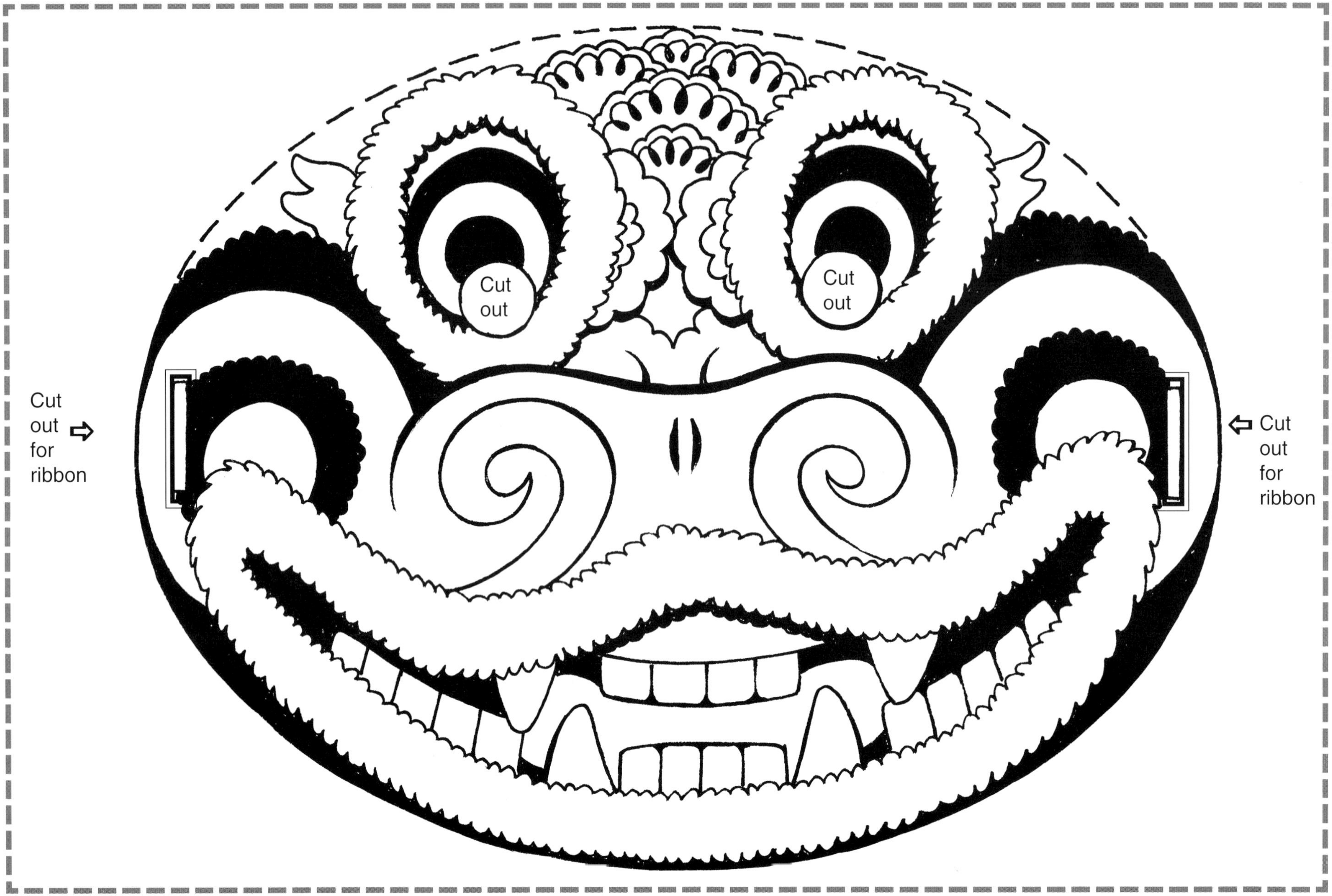

Cut
out
for
ribbon ⇨

Cut
out

Cut
out

⇦ Cut
out
for
ribbon

Bunny boxes

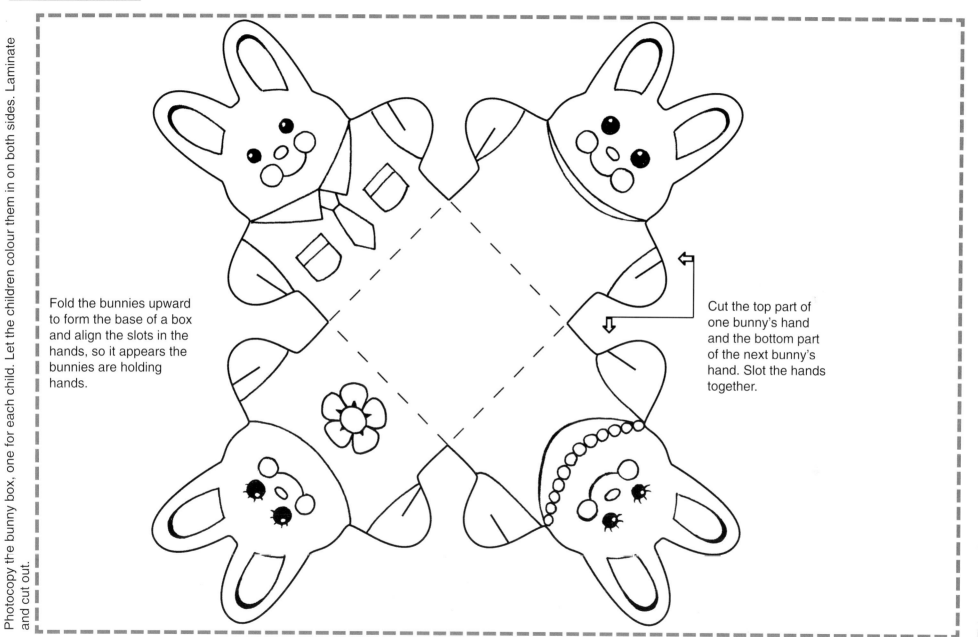

Fold the bunnies upward to form the base of a box and align the slots in the hands, so it appears the bunnies are holding hands.

Cut the top part of one bunny's hand and the bottom part of the next bunny's hand. Slot the hands together.

Photocopy the bunny box, one for each child. Let the children colour them in on both sides. Laminate and cut out.

This page may be photocopied for use by the purchasing institution only.

© Rebecca Taylor
www.brilliantpublications.co.uk

Mathematical Development

It's our tiger's birthday

You will need paper plates to stick this face on to. Photocopy the face/mask onto card and get the children to colour in both the mask and the outside of the plate, see inset. Cut out the mask and glue the tabs on to the plate. Adjust the distance between eye-holes for each child.

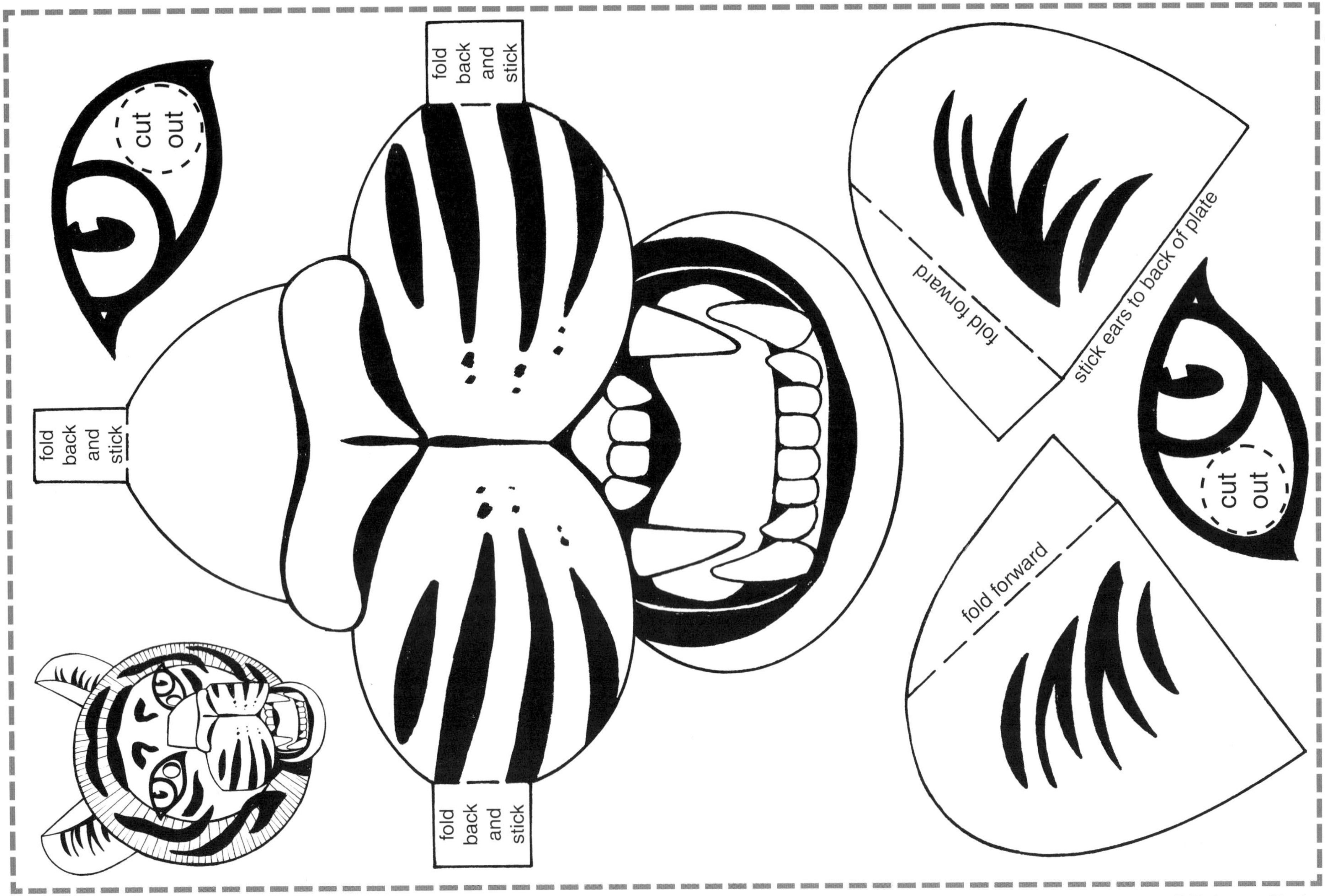

cut out

fold back and stick

fold back and stick

fold back and stick

fold forward

stick ears to back of plate

cut out

fold forward

Mathematical Development

Colourful cube game part 1

finish

start

Colourful cube game part 2

blue

red

blue

yellow

yellow

red

Twist on to a colour

Red	**Yellow**
Blue	**Green**

Mathematical Development

Family journeys

General ideas for your setting area.

Our bear, Ben, likes to go on family holidays.

Our bear went to a farm here.

Daniel took our bear to his Nan's house.

Lucy took Ben to the beach.

LONDON

Claire is borrowing Ben at the moment.

Our Ben's journeys

My family number game part 1

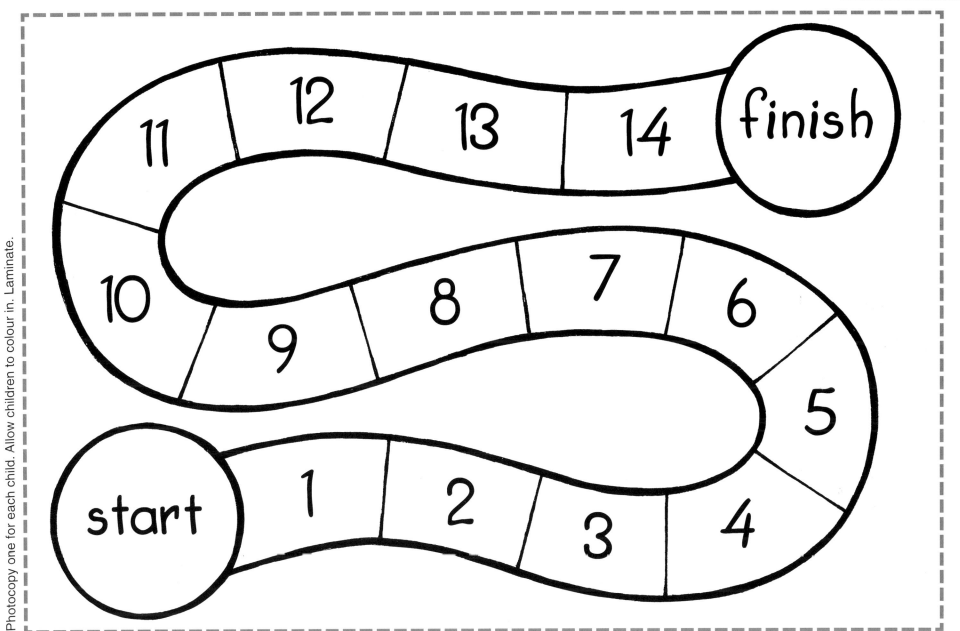

My family number game part 2

Photocopy on to coloured card, laminate while flat and cut out..

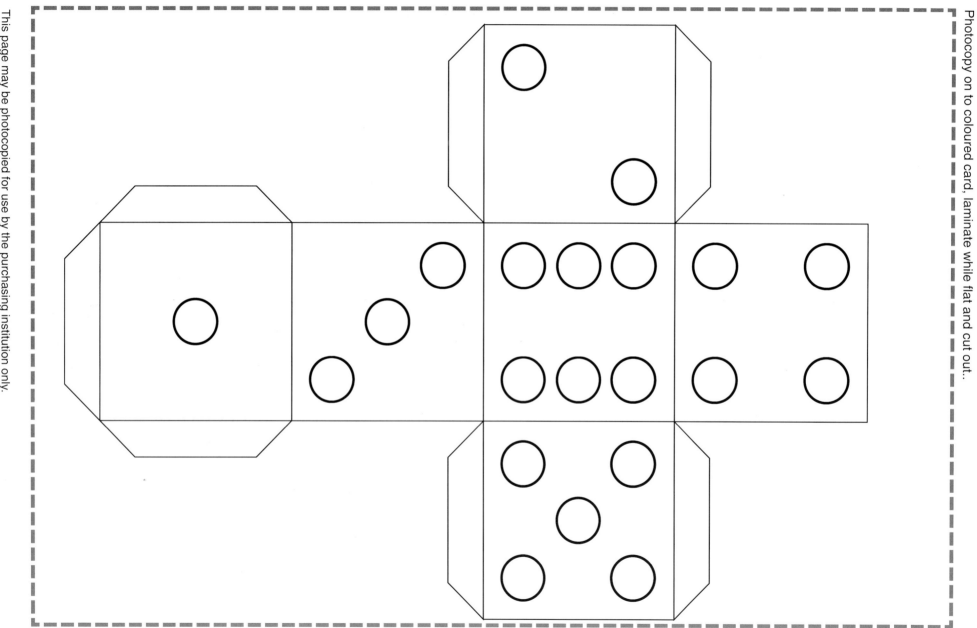

Mathematical Development

Pizza parlour

Ingredients (for one 25 cm pizza)
225 g plain flour
1/2 teaspoon of salt
2 tablespoons of oil
150 ml milk
Toppings
75 g cheese, grated
Tomato puree
Ham
Pineapple
Tuna
Pepperoni

Method
1. Sift the flour and salt together into a big bowl. Make a hole in the centre.
2. Mix the oil and the milk in a jug and pour it into the flour.
3. Using a palette knife or the back of a spoon stir the mix well, until it binds together to make a sticky dough.
4. Sprinkle your worktop and rolling pin with flour, and roll the dough into a circle.
5. Cover with tomato puree and selected toppings, finishing off with a sprinkle of cheese.
6. Bake in the oven for 15–20 minutes at gas mark 6, 200°C or 400°F.

House shape game part 1

Enlarge this page on to A3 thin card. Let the children colour in. Laminate, cut out the shapes, and mount the base board on to card.

House shape game part 2

circle

triangle

hexagon

miss a turn

oblong

square

House bingo

Enlarge this page on to A3 paper. Let the children colour in. Laminate, cut out the shapes, and mount the base board on to card.

Bingo!

1	4	5
3	6	2

Bingo!

1	4	5
3	6	2

Body bingo part 1

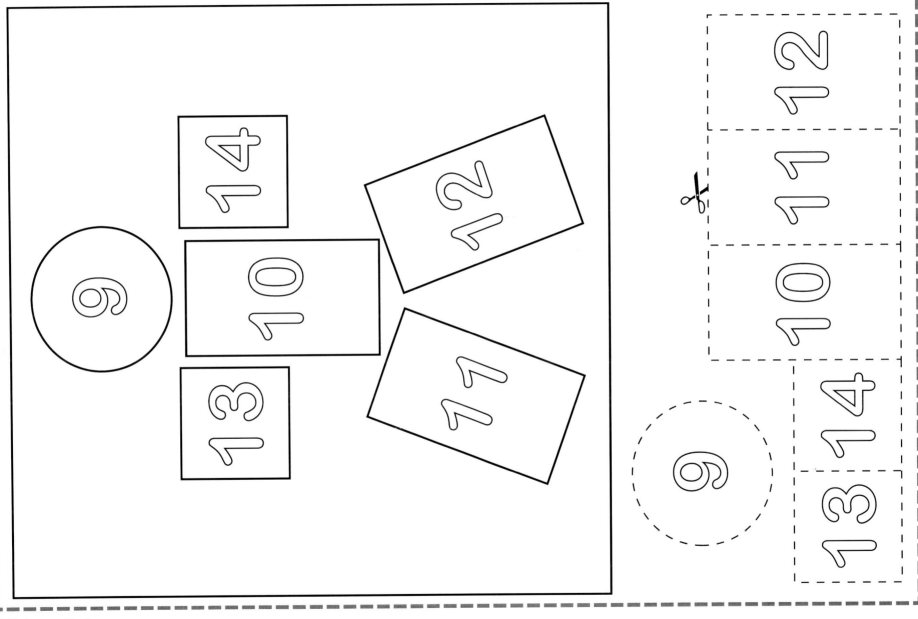

Enlarge this page on to A3 paper. Let the children colour in. Laminate, cut out the shapes, and mount the base board on to card.

Body bingo part 2

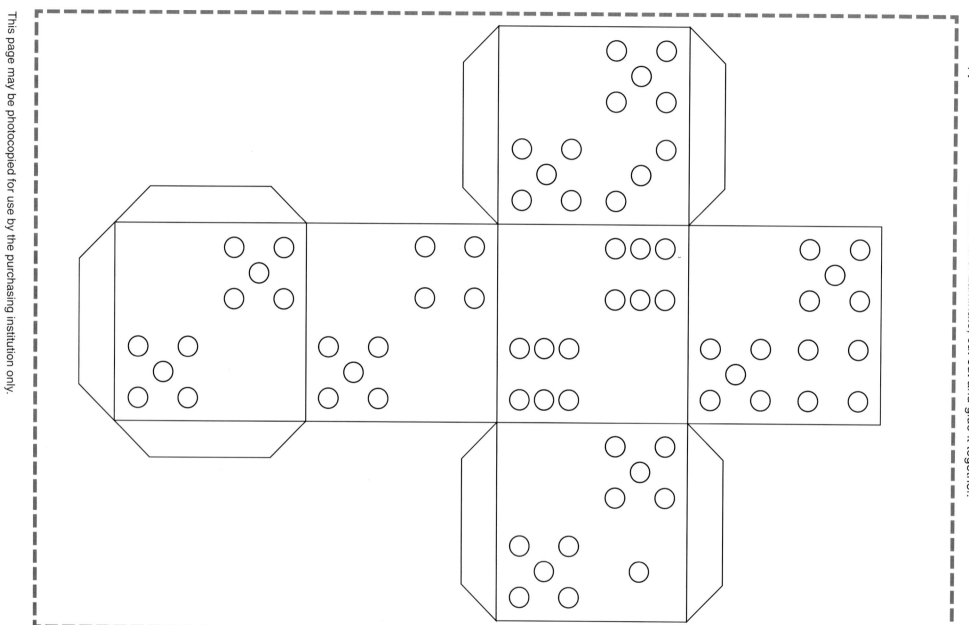

Mathematical Development

Making a moving season wheel

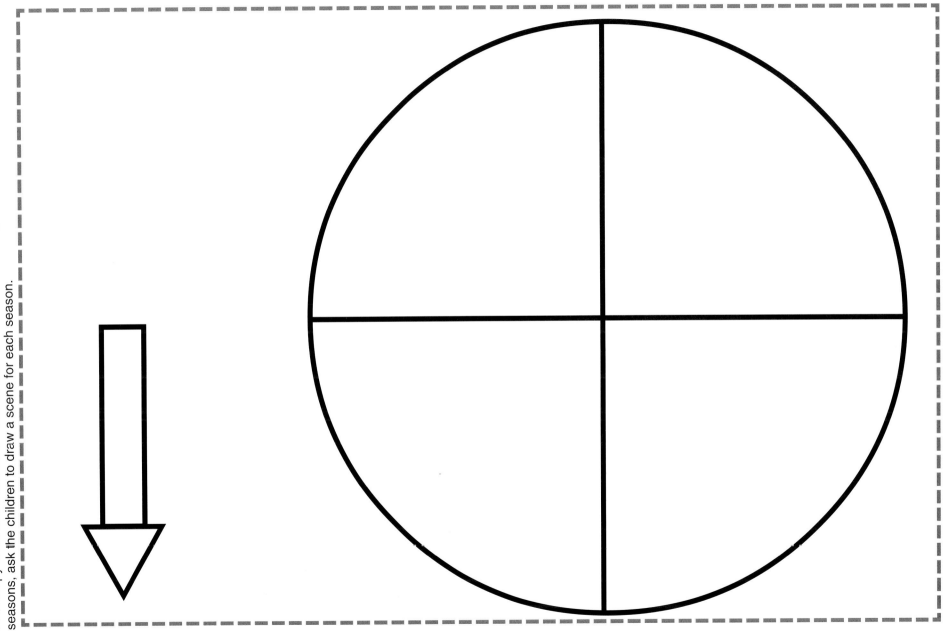

Photocopy on to thin white card – one for each child. After discussing the differences between the seasons, ask the children to draw a scene for each season.

This page may be photocopied for use by the purchasing institution only.

Teddy bear clock

Photocopy bear and arrows. Allow children to colour in. Laminate and cut out. Using a split pin, attach the hands to the centre of the bear.

Mathematical Development

Repeating-pattern toy part 1

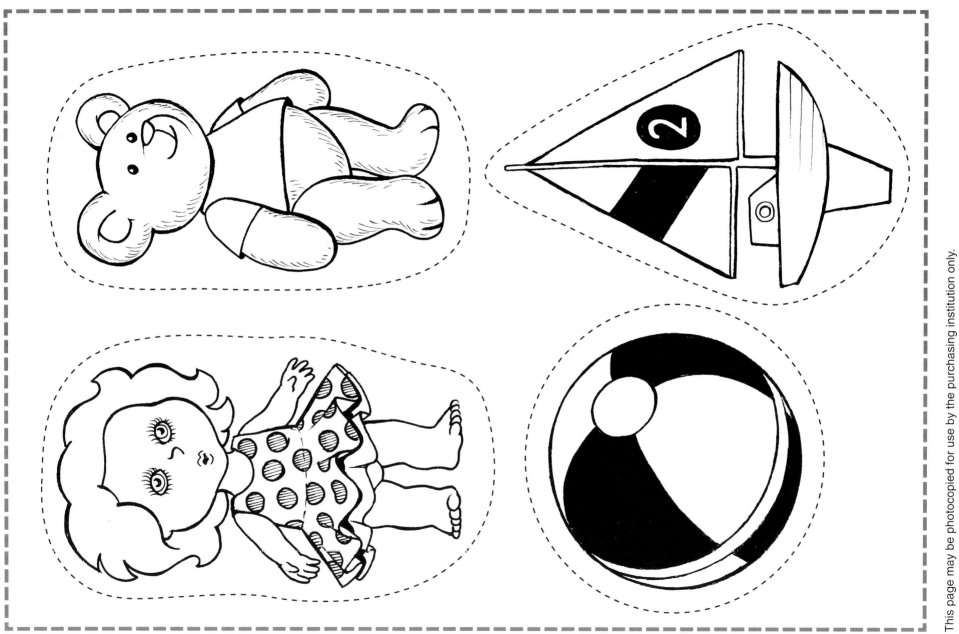

Photocopy these sheets several times for each child. Let the children colour them in. Laminate and cut out shapes. Can the children use these shapes to make a repeating-pattern?

Repeating-pattern toy part 2

Teddy bear paper chain

Fold a strip of sugar paper into a concertina. Photocopy and cut out teddy bear template, place it on top of the sugar paper, making sure that the arms and feet touch the folded edges. Cut out your paper chain and colour it in.

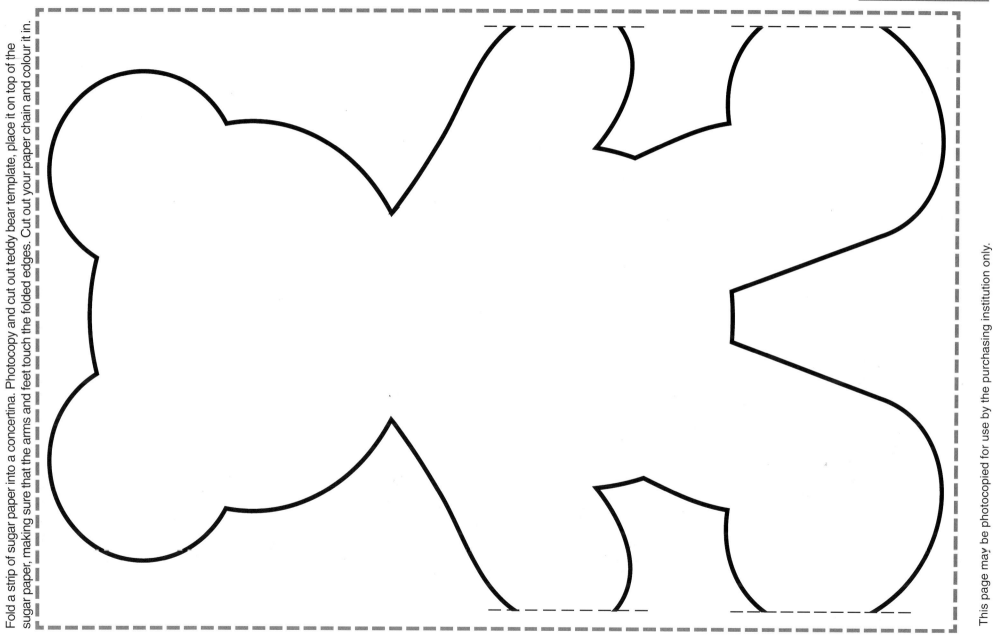

This page may be photocopied for use by the purchasing institution only.

© Rebecca Taylor
www.brilliantpublications.co.uk

Mathematical Development   **143**

Daily weather chart

Mathematical Development